DIGITAL BUSINESS

SHARPEN YOUR EXECUTIVE SKILLS

DIGITIZE,
ANALYZE,
AUTOMATE,
AND OPTIMIZE

GREG GUTKOWSKI

TO MY WIFE MONIKA

Special thanks to Nina Fazio for help with this book.

CONTENTS

INTRODUCTION

From an executive perspective, the digital revolution offers two major benefits. The first is related to new business models such as Airbnb, Amazon, Netflix, or Uber. The second is around the more frequent and granular measurement of all detailed steps and costs associated with all existing business processes.

As the cost of data collection, storage, and transmission becomes almost negligible, there is tremendous potential in streamlining, optimizing, and automating existing business models as much as feasible.

Most businesses are not going to be disrupted *a la* Uber or Airbnb mode. Construction, manufacturing, restaurants, pest control, plumbing, car repair, roofing, landscaping, sports, live entertainment, transportation, and healthcare come to mind. Anything that involves a local physical component is here to stay.

However, not every business is here to stay. The winners will be those that automate all the supporting functions (marketing, sales, service, billing, analysis) and optimize the actual cost of labor, production, and logistics.

If you want to win in 21st century business, you need to digitize, analyze, automate, and optimize. And the best way to do that is to start collecting granular data on 'anything that moves'.

This book will guide you on how to accomplish the goal of maximizing profits via digitization of key business processes. Reading this book will sharpen your executive digital skills.

We will focus on processes that are common to all businesses regardless of size and industry. Every business needs to market, sell, and service customers. These three processes used to be relatively manual and distinctive but are melting into a digitally blended phenomenon called 'customer experience'.

It is getting harder and harder to distinguish where marketing ends, sales start, and customer service starts or ends. In reality, these three processes need to be well aligned and continuously feed each other with information, leads, and profitable relationships. They also need to combine the 'clicks and bricks' or digital and physical aspects of interaction with customers.

The ultimate goal for all businesses is getting and retaining profitable customers. The best practice to achieve this is to analyze as many steps as possible in real time and react quickly, effectively, and efficiently.

Another question is who is going to build and implement the systems and analyze the data to accomplish all of these daunting tasks? The last section of this book discusses the challenges of talent management in times of this digital skills gap in the U.S. labor force.

PART I

MARKETING OVERVIEW

'Marketing is business and business is marketing.'

1

INTRODUCTION

The official definition of marketing as presented by the American Marketing Association reads as follows:

"Marketing is the activity, set of institutions, and processes for creating, communicating, delivering, and exchanging offerings that have value for customers, clients, partners, and society at large. "

This definition is quite broad and rather vague, but it comes from the single largest marketing organization in the world—so it is worth citing here.

Defined as such, it would encompass all human activities today—maybe with the exception of war. And, one can argue that, indeed, most human activities involve exchanging offerings that have value to others.

Philip Kotler, a professor of marketing at Northwestern University, is considered one of the top marketing experts in the world. He defines marketing as follows:

*"Marketing is a social process by which individuals and groups obtain what they **need and want** through creating and exchanging products and value with each other."*

This definition is similar to the AMA's, but more specific, as it addresses needs and wants and thus goes deeper into the depiction of this phenomena.

The fact that the two highest authorities in the field have different definitions of marketing tells us that the discipline we are to learn more about must be quite complex and rather important.

Actually, marketing is as old as human civilization.

It is a derivative of the word 'market', a concept as old as the first time people exchanged goods with each other.

The concept was very simple and still is. When having a surplus, you want to exchange it for something that you could not produce yourself, for whatever reason: lack of time, skills, raw materials, or tools.

So you took your products to the central place in your village or town and you bartered. A chicken for flour, flour for fruit, fruit for vegetables, vegetables for a hammer or a rake, a steer for a couple of goats, etc.

This got a little complex. It's not very convenient to carry steers along as a form of payment, so the Phoenicians invented metal money. After that, trading goods became much easier on many fronts.

The concept of the market has survived very well and it is one of the few common fixtures of any culture, country, region, or city.

Actually, due to the ease of transportation and the 'de facto' common currency of the American dollar, the market is now global; but the concept is as ancient as the human race.

Thus, marketing is as integral to our lives as breathing, eating, working, and playing.

- Breath-ing
- Eat-ing
- Work-ing
- Play-ing
- Market-ing

We will now examine 4 other definitions of marketing in more depth:

- Needs, Wants, Demands
- Marketing mix or 4 Ps
- Peter Drucker's
- The Ultimate Marketing Definition Of Wealth Creation

2

MARKETING DEFINITIONS

There are several competing definitions of marketing. We will be discussing them in more depth here.

For some, "marketing" just means sales. For others "marketing" is frequently associated with just promotions. In many companies "marketing" is in charge of just advertising (mostly via print), social media, procurement of promotional gadgets, and the organization of trade shows.

In this part of our book we address this misconception, which contributes to a misunderstanding of this very important business activity. In a nutshell, we think that marketing is a profitable business, and business is profitable marketing.

Marketing Definition #1

*"Marketing is a social process by which individuals and groups obtain what they need and want through creating and exchanging products and value with each other **based on the demand**."*

Demand is defined here as the ability to pay for what we need or want.

Definition # 1 is a derivative of one proposed by Professor Kotler. I have added a concept of demand to it.

Let's first discussed needs in this context. Examples of needs are basic things such as food to prevent hunger, clothing to protect the body from cold and heat, as well as the basic human needs of safety and procreation.

Few would argue that these are indeed the basic needs that have to be met on an ongoing basis—otherwise people would just perish.

- Food
- Clothing
- Safety
- Procreation

It's human nature that when we are not hungry and feel safe, we want more from life. It is a part of human nature that most of us long for love, but also power, esteem, status, and—for a lot of us—the corresponding conveniences and luxuries that come with them.

Abraham Maslow (1908-1970) was an American psychologist who proposed a famous theory of a hierarchy of human psychological needs. It is represented on this slide. According to Maslow, self-actualization is at the top of the hierarchy.

The components of self-actualization such as morality, creativity, and spontaneity will come in very handy in addressing the overall impact of marketing on the history of the human race—to be discussed later in this chapter.

- Power
- Esteem
- Status
- Convenience
- Luxury

So far, our needs and wants are just wishful thinking if we cannot pay for them. In an extreme example, we will die of hunger or malnutrition if we don't have money for food. This is still happening around the world, especially malnutrition.

In a less dramatic example, we will be frustrated with our inability to pay for a 'wanted' $15K Rolex watch or a $3,000 bottle of French wine.

Thus, from the perspective of providing goods and services, it is not enough that someone needs or wants something. They have to be able to pay for it for other people to provide it. Their 'wants' need to be supported by the purchasing power.

This is very important to the overall concept and driver of wealth creation, to be discussed later in this chapter.

Imagine the world without the following 'wants'. Only 100 years ago most humans could not even imagine (not speaking of wanting or needing) the following items:

- Cars with automatic transmission
- Airplanes
- Electricity at home
- Radio
- Internet
- Computers
- Phones
- TV
- Cameras
- Cruise control
- GPS
- Air conditioning
- Video games

I think, today most of us would classify them as 'needs'— not even 'wants' :-)

Marketing Definition #2

This brings us to yet another definition of marketing. This one is devoid of wants and needs and self-actualization. It concentrates on a prosaic mix of ingredients for marketing success; i.e.:

Product, Price, Place, and Promotion

It is worth noting that this definition complements the previous one, as product can be designed and promoted based on Maslow's hierarchy of needs. This definition is just more operational in scope.

- Marketing Mix or 4 Ps
  - Product
  - Price
  - Place
  - Promotion

The product is defined here as a tangible or intangible.

Intangibles would include, for example, the service of tax preparation. Politics and politicians are examples of marketing ideas; and visits to a nature center or national park would be examples of an experience.

All aspects of product design such as look, feel, colors, warranties, return policies, and what constitutes, for example bronze or silver or gold level packages would belong to this category.

- Item satisfying needs or wants
  - Tangible or intangible (service, ideas, or experience)
  - Service level (bronze, silver, gold packages)
  - Design, packaging, warranties, returns

Price is defined here as the amount of money exchanged for a product or service. The price could just be based on the cost of producing the goods (plus mark-ups), or it could be based on the perceived value. One great example of perceived value is a $3000 ticket for a front row seat at an NBA game, or $20 million for a painting. In both cases, the actual value ignores the actual cost, which could be around $20. Needless to say, one would expect to make much more money on the latter than the former.

- Amount paid for product or service
  - Based on cost
  - Based on perceived value

A 'place' is defined here as to how and where a customer can obtain the offering. This will include considerations such as online versus a physical store, via distributors only, etc. It would also take into consideration the transport and warehousing of tangible goods.

- Where and how customers can get it
  - Brick and mortar stores
  - Online
  - Via distributors
  - Transport and warehousing

Marketing communications include ad copy, a magazine article, or social media posts, with corresponding frequencies, venues, and occasions.

- Marketing communication
  - What is the message
  - Mix of advertising, trades shows, and public relations
  - Message frequency

Marketing Definition #3

"Marketing is so basic that it cannot be considered a separate function. It is the whole business…" Peter Drucker

I have to admit that I like Peter Drucker's definition of marketing the most.

I agree with him that it is impossible to separate the function of a business from marketing. Marketing is business and business is marketing. It's as simple as that. You have no business if you cannot market it; i.e., if you don't have customers.

Every activity of the business should be focused on only two tasks: getting and retaining profitable customers. HR, Accounting, IT, purchasing, etc. are just supporting roles to get more customers and treat existing ones royally.

Unfortunately, in large and currently successful companies, it's easy to lose focus and fall in love with our own brilliance, which breeds arrogance. Just think of Comcast today :-)

Some companies have so much inertia due to their sheer size and previous success that it is easy to forget what drives their business. As a result, existing customers are abused and new customers may not have a choice (Comcast again, being a perfect example while enjoying a monopoly in certain markets). Nevertheless, ignoring existing customers and treating new ones as a nuisance is not a sustainable strategy for any business, and Comcast will have to change or it will perish with 5G technologies just around the corner :-) Just think Blockbuster, Kodak, Motorola, or Encyclopedia Britannica of yesteryear.

"The business of America is business" said Calvin Coolidge

I think that Calvin Coolidge, the 30th President of the United States, was a great marketer of… America. He got it right and he got support from the other side of the political aisle many years later when…President's Clinton economic adviser, James Carville coined a campaign phrase: "It's the economy, stupid!"

We often don't realize how instrumental marketing and business are to our economy and wealth.

During the lifetimes of Coolidge and Carville, the average wealth of an American citizen grew 8 times!

How did we increase the size of Gross Domestic Product per capita almost -8-fold in 100 years?

The answer is pretty simple. We did it by applying principles of marketing! Here is a list of more detailed steps:

1. New technology or service saves time, hence labor, hence cost
2. The price of a given product goes down
3. More people have more money to spend

4. Since people love to spend when they can afford it, they create demand for more products and services—often luxuries or near-luxuries
5. New products and services are introduced - as inventors and investors see the opportunity to make money
6. Back to #1, times the number of new products, which gives us a multiplier of wealth creation

Here are some other great statistics about the same forces working globally— not just in the United States

Since 1820 till today

-   The percentage of people living in extreme poverty decreased from over 90% to 10%
-   Illiteracy has shrunk from 90% to 17%
-   Child mortality declined from 45% to 4%
-   The percentage of people living in democracies increased from 1% to 55%

3

SUCCEEDING IN MARKETING

You may ask what it takes to succeed in marketing. Let's discuss this first from an individual perspective. We will cover risk-taking, the desire to pursue happiness, and creativity.

Starting a new business or introducing new products is very risky. On average, about 8 out of 10 new businesses fail within the first 18 month of operation, which means that only 20% make it.

Only 4% of businesses survive 10 years.

The reasons range from poor timing, wrong location, lack of capital, lack of understanding of the market, wrong partners, etc. All 4 P's can go wrong - product, price, promotion, place.

The majority of marketing decisions (especially during the startup phase) cannot be supported by analytics only and are based on experience, gut feeling, intuition, vision, personal IQ, ambition, and desires. In a nutshell, many things can go wrong with some of them under your control and some of them completely out of it (such as the housing collapse in 2008).

Therefore, having tolerance for risk taking is one of the most important personal traits. Starting a new business or introducing a new product is a gamble.

Next is the desire to pursue happiness (however defined). In most cases, this is happiness related to the personal and financial freedom that a successful business can bring to your life. You can also call it ambition. You will need a lot of creativity to solve such a challenging puzzle involving the alignment of so many moving parts in time and space. And the moving parts will range from a mundane extension of office space to strategic planning and securing funding from demanding investors.

A lot of things in marketing are very ambiguous, meaning debatable, obscure, imprecise, vague, dubious, and uncertain. If you are not comfortable dealing with ambiguity, then marketing is probably not the best career path for you.

There will be a lot of problems to solve, starting with the definition of a problem you are trying to solve for your customers with your products. If you get it wrong, you will not survive for long.

Thus, a lot of innovation will be most useful, as many of the problems you will face you have no experience dealing with in the past.

Last but not least, you will need to be able to articulate your vision, value, strategy, and tactics to prospective customers, existing clients, and to your staff and investors. Very good communication skills are a must.

Our discussion on what it takes to succeed in marketing may explain why the best high school or college students are not always the most successful business people.

In school, you are mostly graded on your cognitive and memorization capabilities plus the discipline to attend on a fixed schedule. As we have demonstrated above, these are not the top three requirements to make it big in the business world. These are top requirements to succeed in science instead...which does not require dealing with so many moving parts while risking your income.

The school of life beyond college will grade you on business capabilities if you decide to pursue this exciting career :-)

Think about Columbus—the ultimate marketer. It took a lot of ambition, dealing with risk and ambiguity plus superior salesmanship to convince the Spanish queen to pay for his expedition. As a result of his brave actions, he made a permanent name for himself in history and impacted the turn of human events for centuries to come.

There is also a societal component to business success. For example, in the not too distant past, running a store, factory or any business was not valued by society as it is now in the United States. In the class societies, societal esteem and prestige accrued to aristocracy and nobility living off land granted by a king or queen.

Shopkeepers, accountants, businessmen, lawyers, and factory owners were treated socially as second class citizens despite their wealth. A poor aristocrat who lost his estate in a drunken card game had more social prestige than a wealthy, hard-working factory owner putting in 12 hours a day at his business.

As you can imagine, Europe was hardly fertile ground for entrepreneurship and business building for most of the 19th and 20th centuries. Nor was the rest of the world that was still stuck in class societies.

It also helps when social and fiscal policies reward business building by letting you keep more of what you have earned. With a very high tax on income and inheritance, individuals are less likely to work extra hard just to pay taxes.

It is also hard to expect innovation and creativity in a society fighting class warfare by stigmatizing wealth creation and the success of individuals….but this is a topic for a political science class :-)

Therefore, not surprisingly, the business of marketing is not compatible with high taxation and regulation, systemic corruption, a lack of personal freedoms (especially freedom of speech), and collectivism. Such environments go against the Maslow hierarchy of needs. Such systems do not reward risk-taking, the pursuit of happiness, and creativity.

Ask yourself this question: How many inventions, new products, and scientific discoveries have been introduced by oppressive regimes around the world?

Guess where the following products and services have been invented and then spread around the world?

Air bag	Air Condition	Aircraft carrier	Assembly line
ATM	Baby food	Barbed wire	Barcode
Bifocal lenses	Blood bank	Blow dryer	Brassiere (bra)
Breakfast cereal	Calculator	Cash register	Cat litter
Chewing gum	Computer games	Credit card	Crossword puzzle
Defibrillator	Deodorant	Dishwasher	Disposable diapers
DNA	E-mail	Electric car	Electric motor
Elevator	Escalator	First agricultural combine	First Cell phone
First commercial airplane	First database	First power plant electrifying a city	First TV station
Frozen food	Genetic engineering	GPS	Grocery coupons
Home smoke detector	Internet	Laser	Laundromat
Light bulb	Lipstick tube	Mail order catalog	Microwave oven

Motion picture	Nylon	Oral contraceptive	Petroleum
Potato chips	Refrigerator	Remote control	Revolver
Revolving doors	Richter scale	Roller coaster	Rubber for tires
Satellite	Skyscraper	Sliced bread	Stapler
Steamboat	Sunscreen	Supermarket	Tampon
Tea bag	Telephone	Toilet paper	Toothpaste
Tractor	Traffic lights	Typewriter	Ultrasound for obstetrics
Viagra	Video tape	Virtual reality	Zipper

All of the above originated as business products or services in the U.S.A. – the most in the last 100 years.

As an interesting phenomena, it's is worth noting the impact of military technologies on business. Throughout history, civilian and military technologies have been supporting each other and contributing to wealth creation.

Here are some examples of recent U.S. military technologies that became the basis for common products and many businesses worldwide:

Internet	Laser	GPS	Databases
Motion sensors	Computer Mouse	Windows as computer interface	Computer maps
Voice Recognition	Satellites	Unix operating system	Drones & Microwave ovens

What Does It Take To Succeed in Marketing?

- Tolerance for risk taking
    - Societal
    - Individual
- Desire to pursue happiness
- Creativity
- Ambiguity
- Problem solving
- Innovation
- Articulation
- Rewards for risk taking
    - Keeping what you've earned
    - Social esteem

4

MARKETING CRITICISM

Let's address some commonly heard criticisms of the business of marketing.

The one I hear a lot is that 'marketers create needs that nobody needs'.

Human needs for food, safety, love and esteem cannot be created; they are inherent in being human.

Existing products only fulfill these needs to a better or worse effect based on individual income.

- 'Marketers create needs'
  - o Needs already exist - one cannot create a need
  - o Products/services satisfy existing needs

Another popular criticism is that 'marketers get people to buy what they don't want'

The last time I checked, the United States is a free country. Nobody forces anyone to buy anything. The exceptions are government mandated car and health insurance and a variety of building permits. So don't blame private business :-)

In a free country, with free speech, anyone has a right to influence new 'wants'. As demonstrated earlier, the 'wants' are the drivers of continuous wealth creation that benefits the whole society.

- 'Marketers get people to buy what they don't want'
- It's a free country, nobody forces anyone to buy anything (with the exception of car and health insurance and a variety of permits, which are not marketing mechanisms)
- Marketers have a right to influence new wants

Also, as we demonstrated earlier, the poor are not getting poorer. They get richer and so do the rich, who get *even* richer as well. We can debate who gets more of the surplus, but all of us became more affluent in the last 100 and even 50 years due to the creativity of businesses.

Also, the definition of 'poor' is highly debatable. If I am making a minimum wage while living with parents, driving their car, and going to college, does it make me poor? By some official statistics – of course!

On the other hand, when I get a good job after graduation, do I become instantly rich?

It is very interesting who and how one decides what constitutes poverty and affluence. I suspect that this is a prerogative of 'rich' politicians doing a market segmentation for the maximum number of votes in their districts :-)

Exploitation

Exploitation is based on a mathematical term called a zero sum game. This means that one person's gain is equivalent to another's loss, so the net change in wealth is zero.

The best example is a land invasion and occupation by an enemy army. The amount of land is the same, but the gain of the invading country is equal to the loss of the invaded one.

Robbing a bank is probably the most obvious example.

Football, basketball, and soccer are great examples of a zero sum game as well. For one team to win, another has to lose while the total pool of rewards remains the same.

The same goes for sharing a pizza with friends. The more you get, the less they get; but the total calorie intake is the same.

- Territorial expansion - if I got your land, you lost yours
- Robbing a bank - a robber got more money, the bank lost
- Sports - for one to win, another has to lose
- Sharing a single pizza - if I get a bigger slice, yours is smaller

Zero Sum Game?

Here is a classic example where the zero sum game concept is completely irrelevant and everyone involved gets richer.

Bill Gates made $ billions by creating and selling software. Did he take that wealth from someone else? Or did he create **ADDITIONAL** value that people were willing to pay for?

He did not force anyone at a gunpoint to buy Excel. He faced stiff competition from Quattro Pro, Lotus 1-2-3, and VisiCalc.

Did his customers get their money's worth? Yes they did. Did they do it voluntarily? Yes they did.

Imagine doing accounting or numeric analysis by hand today. Society got much more productive analyzing numbers and it was willing to pay for it. More productivity generated more wealth and demand for new products and so on as we already discussed as a cycle of wealth creation.

- Bill Gates made $ billions by creating and selling software
- Did he take that wealth from someone else?

- Or did he create **ADDITIONAL** value that people were willing to pay for?
- Did his customers get their money's worth? *Imagine doing accounting by hand.*

Poor getting poorer? The income gap is growing?

In this example, let's say that today, you make $50K per year and your boss is making $100K. The difference is $50K or 100%.

In five years, your company is growing, both of you have more experience and now you are making $100K and your boss is making $200K. Oh, my gosh! The difference grew to $100K—this is not fair, this is exploitation, you may think. But wait, the percentage difference is still the same. Your boss still makes twice as much as you do.

So the income gap grew in terms of actual dollars, but both of you are making much more money now that your boss is making only twice as much as you do, exactly like 5 years before.

Another observation—in 15 years your boss will retire and his or her income will be much less than yours, while you will be enjoying the peak of your earning power. So the rich will get poorer, too…eventually :-)

- Year 1 - you make $50 K - your boss makes $100K - difference $50K or 100%
- Year 5 - you make $100K - your boss makes $200K - difference $100K, still 100%
- Did your boss get richer and you got poorer?
- Or did the two of you get richer?
- … while your boss still makes twice as much as you do.

Now after we've addressed several popular economic misconceptions about the role of business, let's talk about the confusion around marketing as a term.

Very often, it is unintentionally confused with the following terms:

- Business
- Sales
- Advertising
- Promotions
- Public relations
- Commerce
- International trade
- Inventions
- Entrepreneurship
- Economics— the branch of knowledge concerned with the production, consumption, and transfer of wealth.

Let's address them one at a time.

As discussed before, Business is Marketing and Marketing is Business. We will be using these terms interchangeably throughout the book.

Sales is a subset of marketing and belongs to the 'Place' category among the 4Ps. It is an act of displaying, informing, and persuading to acquire the product.

The most confusion is around the distinction between marketing and advertising, which are often used interchangeably. Advertising is 'Promotion' - one of the 4Ps.

The same goes for Promotions.

Public relations is the marketing of ideas and a subset of Promotions. The concept is to influence the public by working with the media to make them aware of your activities without paying directly for advertising.

Commerce as a term is interchangeable with business and marketing. Sometimes commerce is understood more as an act of selling and buying large quantities—but not always. I think 'commerce' sounds more sophisticated than 'business', so we have the Department of Commerce and not the Department of Business or the Department of America :-)

Trade and International Trade - same as commerce. Trade, commerce, marketing, business are all interchangeable in the context of this book.

Inventions are part of the 'Product' category of the 4P's definition.

Entrepreneurship is interchangeable with the startup phase of any business.

Economics deals with production, consumption, and transfer of wealth by the whole society and as such encompasses external factors such as politics, monetary policy, international trade agreements, and taxation, which are beyond the control of a business person. So 'business' is a subset of 'economics'.

5

MARKETING IN HISTORY

I think that the history of the world and the history of business are inseparable. The development of our civilization and therefore the history of the human race have always been driven by the desire to get more out of life (whatever the definition of 'more' involved). If we subscribe to Maslow's theory of the hierarchy of human desires, that should not be surprising.

New inventions were always used to either increase wealth by increasing productivity, or as new weapons to conquer and defend. There has been a constant exchange between military and civilian technologies impacting each other as previously discussed.

As an old Roman proverb says, 'if you want peace, prepare for war'. Wars are won on intelligence and logistics, so you better have good products and services, both civilian and military.

The history of human civilization has not always been rosy. Humans have learned only very recently that making trade, not war, is a much better way to coexist in this world.

Even today, not all regimes subscribe to this notion; but as demonstrated before, the world is safer and healthier in general as we do business with each other, rather than wage war.

The human race has learned that traditional slavery is not viable. Neither is the slavery of fascism or communism. The world is now connected like never before, not only with the Internet but also with many trade treaties that make wars less likely.

I believe that the more people understand that, the more we can all grow more affluent without exploitation, and the less likely there will be electoral support for military 'adventures' around the whole world.

Let's not be naive and think that the road ahead of us is without trouble. But the amount of trouble will decrease with an increased knowledge of business, marketing, and economic issues. Thus, the future of the world is inseparable from marketing.

6

MARKETING INDUSTRY

Depending on the definition of marketing, the share of business as a percent of our Gross Domestic Product is between 50 and 70 percent.

About 20 percent comprise government functions and services, and about 15% is health care. But keep in mind that both government and healthcare use a lot of public relations, advertising, and promotional services and products.

The amount of money spent on all TV, print, radio, and online ads in 2016 was about $200 billion. These are only fees paid to various media to advertise and exclude the cost to produce and manage ads campaigns, which is estimated to be another $200 billion. In comparison, the total size of the American economy was about $18 trillion in the same year of 2016.

- Single largest industry
- Local, national, global
- Around 50%-70% of GDP
- Around 25%-35% if defined as promotions and sales
- Government is about 20%

Careers in Marketing

Your career in marketing will most likely start with research analyst, digital marketing specialist, or sales representative. All are great entry ways to learn and understand the business.

As a digital marketing specialist, you may be responsible for the mechanics of running social media posting, email, and search optimization campaigns. The natural progression will lead to a role as a product/program/communication manager, or a sales manager on the selling side.

There is a growing category of data analysts who specialize in managing and analyzing data to support decision making.

I would strongly advise that you assess your skills and aptitudes to select the most desirable concentration. Careers in marketing span a wide variety of skills and talents, and the sooner you know where you would enjoy succeeding and where your best chances are, the better for all involved.

- Market research analyst
- Digital marketing specialist
- Sales rep
- Product managers
- Program managers
- Product designers

It is also very likely that you will work for a digital marketing agency. There is a growing trend toward the division of labor and specialization, especially in smaller businesses. As small businesses lack the scale to hire and retain top talent, they will rely more on marketing agencies as business partners. This will be a similar relationship as smaller businesses have with CPAs or lawyers.

- Marketing Agencies
- Advertising Agencies
- Digital Marketing Agencies

- PR Agencies

Actually there is another trend of traditional management consulting companies getting into the business of digital marketing. This trend supports our observation that business is marketing and marketing is business. It is just harder and harder to distinguish what constitutes business versus marketing consulting. To make it even more interesting, the digital component of marketing forces reliance on technical folks who are even harder to find and retain.

Hence, the fusion of management, marketing, and technical consulting existing under one roof.

- Merging with Management Consulting Agencies
- Driven by digital components
- McKinsey, Deloitte, Boston Consulting,
- Accenture, IBM, PwC

It is hard to predict all job categories that will arise in the future, as they will keep changing over time along with technological change.

But it is not hard to predict what skills will make you a winner. My prediction is that **the future belongs to creative, analytical inter-disciplinarians.**

Sam Walton was one of them. If he were alive today, he would be worth more than Bill Gates or Jeff Bezos by a factor of 2 or 3.

What he did was classic; he quickly recognized the potential and applied emerging digital technologies to the unglamorous business of a discount department store. He was creative, analytical, and interdisciplinary. He saw the potential of technology in the automation of processes such as shipments, payments, reordering, etc.

7

THE ULTIMATE MARKETING DEFINITION

This brings us to the 4th and my own definition of marketing.

Marketing is:

Knowing your customers and customers knowing you while generating wealth in the process

Please, note that none of the previous marketing/business definitions mentioned wealth, profit, or money.

Keep in mind that your ultimate job as a marketer is to make profit.

Without sustainable profit—that is, wealth generation—you will lose your job and/or your business.

Your job as a marketer is to understand all the levers of profit generation. In the past, it was not easy to do as the cost and mechanics of measurement may have been prohibitive. Today, however, inexpensive technologies come to the rescue.

Currently, it is impossible to run a successful company using processes not supported by software. Even if the process is manual, it should be accounted for by tagging it in a digital way. For example, while a construction business may itself be mostly based on manual labor, it would be beneficial to record a time stamp for each step of the way, including the duration of preparation, logistics, and actual labor. And, it would be useful to record all the granular costs associated with each step.

The more granular the capture of relevant data, the more opportunities to increase effectiveness, efficiency, automation and profitability. The better the data, the better the analysis of gaps and opportunities.

Many business processes today may already come with a lot of timestamps reflecting the key components of a process. The best example is communication via email. We know when each email was sent to whom, who was copied or blind-copied, and who opened and/or responded when. We may not have all this data in one single convenient file for analysis, but at least it is already collected. However, the time to compose the body of email and the cost associated with it is not always collected - with the exception of most law practices.

Another common business process with a lot of digital timestamps already in place is found in call centers. We know the start and stop time of each call, who called whom, who hung up, and who put whom on hold.

There are a lot of other processes that may already be highly digitized: digital marketing, sales, customer support, manufacturing, shipping, and accounting. Nevertheless, even if they are digitized, they may not be connected with each other to allow for analysis of overall profitability. For that you may need to combine each step of the process that starts with product promotion and ends in a profit (which may or may not materialize until many months or years later).

In the following chapters we will be discussing in detail how to digitize, analyze, and automate common business processes such as promotions, sales, customer experience, and talent management.

PART II

PROMOTIONS
Digital Marketing

1

INTRODUCTION

Digital marketing can be quite confusing! Digital marketing is a multi-disciplinary blend of traditional methods combined with the never-ending changes in Internet technologies--a lot of data and analytics. There are many interconnected parts, a wide variety of tools, and so many alternatives for putting them together. No wonder many companies find this maze frustrating!

However, this is a great opportunity to turbo-charge your traditional marketing with the latest and greatest digital tools and processes.

In fact, digital marketing is the *least* expensive way to grow your business. With the right application of our digital marketing framework and proven, repeatable processes, this daunting task can be made doable and it could even be a lot of fun. Let us show you how!

The main objective is not to make you an instant expert in digital marketing, but rather to equip you with the knowledge to ask the right questions when working with other team members--including your digital marketing service providers.

After you read this part, you will be positioned to make better decisions on:

- Digital marketing strategy
- What to measure and how to analyze results

- Effective allocation of resources and budgets across a growing number of digital channels
- Planning, implementing, analyzing, and continually improving your Digital Marketing
- Managing service providers

2

DIGITAL MARKETING INTRODUCTION

The section is based on our digital marketing framework, which is made up of various digital channels such as online paid ads, social media, email marketing, and search engine optimization.

Each of the channels has its distinct role, but the idea is to exploit the synergy of using the right mix of digital tools and methods.

We will discuss how digital marketing should support and work with your traditional marketing practices to expand your business.

The challenge is determine which digital channels are relevant to your business and how to allocate resources among all of them.

First, in the Foundations chapter, we introduce the major industry players and their respective roles, and we discuss the most recent trends. We talk a little about the history of digital marketing and the driving forces behind it.

Next we introduce our Digital Marketing Framework, made up of various channels such as online paid ads, search engine optimization, social media, and email.

Following that, we will demonstrate how you can find out what your competition is doing online. Since everyone's website is in the public domain, and with the right tools, we can learn a lot about the digital strategies of our competitors.

After that, you will learn how to calculate your company's technical Internet Readiness Index. We will show you tools and methods to evaluate your existing Internet presence. This will be the basis for identifying critical technical weaknesses that you may not even be aware of!

Equipped with all this knowledge, you can start working on your strategy and a detailed digital marketing plan. You will receive a Digital Marketing template and we will start working on filling it out with specific tasks and budgets. When you return to your office, you will have a solid foundation for an actionable plan to be shared with your team.

One of the advantages of digital marketing is that we can measure the impact of each marketing campaign. Every click by every user is stored and can be analyzed. This allows us to analyze the effectiveness of various programs, channels, and marketing alternatives with a precision unheard of just a few years ago. This leads to better resource allocation and to better marketing in general. Nevertheless, setting up the measurement process is easier said than done. It involves organizing data and knowing how to analyze it by leveraging the most user-friendly tools. We'll show you how to set up your analytics for the best return on investment.

Last but not least, we will discuss the need to integrate all your software and data tools. On average, there are at least 6 major data systems that need to be integrated for real time online analysis. The lack of such integration translates into lost time on manual tasks or missed opportunities to spot a favorable trend or to be warned about a lurking danger.

All of the chapters are supported with real-life case studies from around the world.

This will equip you with unparalleled tools, methods, and resources to formulate your own digital marketing strategy!

3

FOUNDATIONS

In the first exciting chapter, we'll discuss the foundations of digital marketing.

We'll talk about:

- Driving Forces
- Major Players
- Recent trends in this very fast-changing industry

Let's talk about the driving forces behind the digital marketing phenomenon and what's driving the relentless changes in marketing technologies.

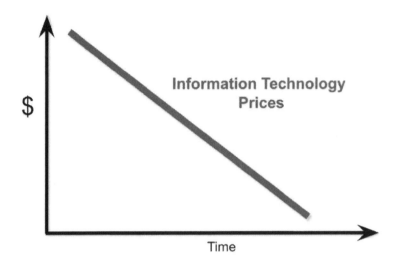

This simple chart provides an explanation for the single largest "driver" of never-ending changes in technologies.

It is the never-ending decrease in the price of information technology.

I know of nothing comparable in the history of humanity that keeps providing more for less.

Gordon Moore, the Co-founder of Intel, predicted this trend in 1965.

Moore's Law simply states that the number of transistors per square inch on integrated circuits had doubled every year since the integrated circuit was invented.

Most experts, including Moore himself, expect this law to hold for at least another two decades.

Translation: Computing power doubles every year without a price increase

Can you even imagine what's yet to come?

So, if you wanted to get the same computing power in 1991 that you have on your iPhone today, you would have had to pay $3.5 million!

The Apollo mission to the moon had less computing power than an average iPhone today.

	1991	2016
1 GB of hard disk storage	$10,000	$0.04
1 GB of flash memory	$45,000	$0.55
Mid-level iPhone with 32GB flash memory + telco	$3,500,000	$350.00

Our table shows that 1 gigabyte of hard disk storage cost $10,000 in 1991. Now it's 4 cents.

1 gigabyte of flash memory was a whopping $45,000. Now you can have it for about 50 cents.

Thus, on average, the cost of comparable computing power today is orders of magnitude less than what it was in 1991. 1/10,000th, to be exact. Pretty amazing, isn't it?

Let's assume that in 1991, a nice Corvette cost about $30,000 and it was getting 15 miles per gallon.

If we were to use the 10,000 ratio of price decrease since 1991, a nice Corvette would cost us 3 dollars today and we would be getting 150,000 miles per gallon.

This very rapid decrease in hardware, software, and telecommunication costs has enabled the collection, movement, storage, and real time analysis of massive amounts of data at a reasonable cost

The concept of **Big Data** was born.

In just the last 10 years, this made possible the creation of, among others

- Facebook – with its 1.7 billion users worldwide
- Google – that gets billions of queries daily
- GPS technologies that track millions of locations in any given moment
- YouTube – where millions of videos are uploaded daily

According to Amit Singhal, Senior Vice President of Google Search, in 2012:

- Google's search engine found more than **30 trillion** unique URLs on the Web
- It crawls **20 billion** sites a day
- Processes **3.5 billion** searches per day

This was not technically feasible in 1991, and even if it were, it would have been prohibitively expensive.

We collect so much data that a new measurement unit was needed to depict these staggering amounts.

The new measurement unit is Petabyte.

It's 10 to the power of 15 bytes.

1 PETABYTE	20 million four-drawer filing cabinets filled with text
1 PETABYTE	13.3 years of HD-TV video
1.5 PETABYTES	Size of the 10 Billion photos on Facebook

20 PETABYTES	The amount of data processed by Google per day
20 PETABYTES	Total Hard Drive space manufactured in 1995
50 PETABYTES	The entire written works of mankind from the beginning of recorded history in all languages

To get a better idea of the amount of data behind one Petabyte, try to imagine the amount of data on 223,000 DVDs, each containing about 5 gigabytes.

For reference, the daily Internet traffic is around 700 Petabytes, and Facebook stores approximately 200 Petabytes.

Please note they're approximations.

1 PB is equal to 20 million four-drawer filing cabinets filled with text, or 13.3 years of HD-TV videos. 1.5 PB is the size of the 10 billion photos stored on Facebook. 20 PB is equivalent of the amount of data processed by Google per a day and the total hard drive space manufactured in 1995. 50 PB is the entire written works of mankind from the beginning of recorded history in all languages.

 The very rapid decrease in the cost of hardware, software and telecommunications enabled business models whereby the service is free and the cost of *running* the service is covered by digital advertising.

This is how digital advertising was born…

We'll talk in more detail about the various types of digital advertising later in our book.

That rapid decrease in hardware, software, and telecom costs has also led to:

- The proliferation of smartphones, which themselves are powerful computers with GPS. Today, there are around 200 million smartphones in the U.S.

- Because of this, smartphones led to over half of all searches today originating from these powerful devices. Over 65% of emails are being opened first on smartphones. We're just glued to these devices most of our days.

- Smartphones became so important in digital marketing that, today, one is unlikely to succeed in opening a new restaurant that cannot be easily found on a smartphone.

3.1

MEASUREMENT REVOLUTION

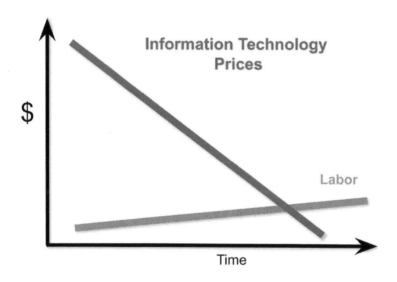

As the price of hardware and software is decreasing, the cost of knowledge workers is increasing, though not at the same rate. However, the cost of professional employees is, for many businesses, the single largest cost of their operations.

Therefore it's very important to equip increasingly expensive professionals with the best tools, especially since the cost of these tools continues to drop.

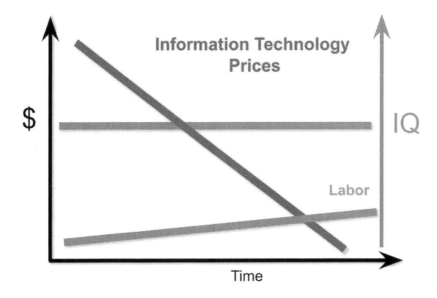

Let's put another dimension on our familiar chart. On the second vertical axis, on the right hand side, we added human IQ-- the *average* human IQ. It is relatively stable and it's not likely to increase much anytime soon.

Therefore, the biggest challenge is how we, as humans, can absorb all these new and continuous changes when our brains have limited capacity to absorb and retain knowledge.

With the right approach and implementation processes, these technological changes can be absorbed and can lead to increased profits. With the wrong approach, they become frustrating and lead to costly mistakes, draining resources and energies.

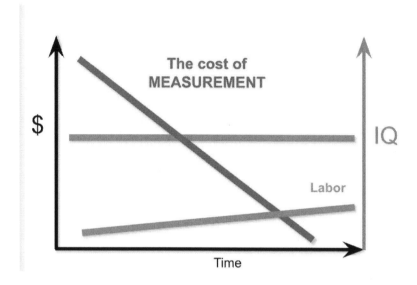

So far, we've talked about the decreasing prices of software and hardware. In the end, they translate to a much lower cost of measurement. We can measure so much more now, and with a precision unimaginable only a few years ago.

In summary: We can count all the clicks on any website every second. We even know the XY coordinates of every click. This is very useful in testing user interfaces, as we can tell where most people click on your page and if they may be confused with a poor website design. We'll cover this in more detail later in the book.

So, we can both measure at very granular levels as well as aggregate massive volumes of data in real time. This translates into real time analytics, which can alert us to unfavorable trends while they're happening.

For example, we can very quickly spot users abandoning a shopping cart for a certain product on a massive ecommerce site.

We're not only in the midst of technological revolution.

We're in the midst of the measurement revolution.

One of the biggest advantages of digital marketing is the ability to analyze massive amounts of data to determine what strategies and channels work the best. We can attribute a single email to a million dollar sale -- if we have the right measurement system in place. We'll discuss in detail how to set up such a measurement system later in our book.

The measurement revolution is a big challenge for traditional marketers who, for the most part, are not big fans of technology and analytics.

Now, the lack of these skills can derail the best creative campaigns.

So keep calm and join the measurement revolution!

Better measurements will set you free ☺

In conclusion - It's not about a lack of technology.

It's not about the price of tools – they're relatively cheap.

But it *is* about our ability to absorb and integrate all these technologies into our marketing processes.

It's about integrating them in such a way that they help to grow the business instead of becoming a frustrating and costly obstacle.

Digital marketing can be confusing and frustrating. Or it could be the least expensive way to grow your business.

3.2

GOLDEN RULES

There are two simple golden rules of digital marketing. If applied, your business will most likely grow.

These two rules are

1. To Find and To Be Found
2. ABC – Attract, Bring, and Convert

The first rule, "To find" and to be found, represents two sides of the same coin. The Internet is a giant digital haystack.

On one hand, you – as a user – want to be able to find what you're looking for very quickly among billions of sites. So you use search engines such as Google, Yahoo, and Bing. You type what you're looking for, and in a matter of seconds you may get your answer.

On the other hand, you want to be *found* – as a business – when prospective customers look for you, don't you?

So how can you help them find you?

How important is it to your business that you're easily found?

What can you do to ensure that you can be found in seconds?

We'll discuss some techniques in great detail soon. They are the heart of digital marketing.

The second golden rule – which is closely related to the first one – is the ABC of digital marketing:

A. For Attract
B. For Bring
C. For Convert

The idea is to attract potential customers to click on your listing in search results. For example, if a prospect is looking for a Green Widget and you are in the green widget business, your company should show up at the top of search engine listings. But it's not enough to rank high. The prospect sees several companies listed, and even if you *are* ranking number one, it does not guarantee they will click on your listing. You have to attract them and you only have about 200 characters to do that.

So keep calm and follow the Golden Rules of digital marketing for easy navigation through the maze of the Measurement Revolution.

We've just completed the first part of the Foundations chapter. We talked about the driving force behind relentless technological changes and how to harness them. The underlying driving force is the never-ending decrease in the price of hardware and software.

The next chapter is about the major industry players – fascinating companies that have built their global empires in less than 10 years.

MAJOR PLAYERS 1

In this section, we'll take a look at the major players of the Internet and digital marketing industries.

Company	Browser	HW/OS	Music	Video	News	ecomm	Search	Social	Paid Ads	Apps
Apple	X	X	X		X				X	X
Alibaba			X			X	X	X	X	X
Samsung		X				X				
Google	X	X	X	X	X	X	X	X	X	X
Facebook					X	X	X	X	X	X
Linkedin					X		X	X	X	
Pinterest							X	X	X	
Microsoft	X	X					X		X	
Yahoo			X		X		X		X	
Amazon			X			X	X		X	
Twitter					X			X	X	

This table shows the major players and the markets they're in. It's a fascinating landscape!

There are 3 players in the browser business – Apple with Safari, Google with Chrome, and Microsoft with Explorer. And with Firefox running on all platforms, we don't see any one of the 3 firms in a position to dominate the market. From the digital marketing perspective, a variety of browsers increases the cost of testing website development, as sites have to look good in all 4 browsers.

As far as hardware and operating systems go, we have 4 major players

- Apple with its own iOS, iPads and iPhones, iBeacons and iWatches
- Samsung with smartphones using Android from Google as the operating system
- Google with Android, Chromebook, and Chromecast
- Microsoft with Windows

If you use smartphone apps as part of your digital marketing mix, you need to support both iOS and Android versions.

In the data and application hosting business, also called cloud services, Amazon's AWS and Microsoft's Azure are the two top players. Actually, it is estimated that Amazon makes more profits from hosting data and applications than with its ecommerce operations.

In the music business, we have Apple, Alibaba, Google's YouTube, Yahoo, and Amazon—with Apple dominating the space with iTunes.

Video is totally dominated by Google's YouTube.

Interestingly, 4 titans are in the news business: Apple has just recently entered that market, with Yahoo, Facebook, LinkedIn, and Twitter already established. Today, Facebook is the leader with major publishers streaming their content inside Facebook feeds – the most recent example being The New York Times.

Amazon dominates e-commerce, but the recent entry of Alibaba into the American market may change that dynamic. You can buy things online with Google and Facebook, but e-commerce does not seem to be their focus.

The very lucrative business of search is completely dominated by Google, but all other players, with the exception of Apple and Samsung, are trying to get some share of this pie.

Facebook and Twitter dominate social media for B2C —Business to Consumer. Google has failed to get its Google+ to be widely used. LinkedIn dominates social media for professionals.

Apple, Alibaba, Google, and Facebook are involved in application development such as games, activity tracking, online ordering, and so on.

Google seems to have a presence in all markets. Everybody but Samsung is in the paid ads business in one-way or another.

From the perspective of a digital marketer, Google has to be followed, observed, and analyzed the most. Their dominance in the search business is not going to erode anytime soon, and Google keeps changing the rules of the game in response to growing pressure from its shareholders for more profits.

The second major force is Facebook. Facebook users are just glued to this platform as measured by time spent by users on their social media platform. In B2C marketing, Facebook will be an integral part of any digital marketing efforts for years to come.

The same is true for LinkedIn in B2B, or Business-to-Business, marketing.

All the titans are competing with each other on many fronts and the picture is very dynamic. Some players enter new segments, such as Apple with the news business. Some players exit, like Microsoft abandoning its Nokia acquisition.

The bottom line is that every one of the major players wants to get as much share of your time by tying you with content and/or hardware. From the financial perspective, today Apple leads the pack with great hardware, apps, and music – and now the news. Sometimes we wonder why they didn't enter the social media business – it would be a natural fit! Maybe Apple will merge with Facebook to challenge Google? Who knows? After all, Microsoft has acquired LinkedIn in 2016.

3.4

MAJOR PLAYERS 2

Apple is the largest company in the world in terms of market capitalization. It's bigger that Exxon Mobil, Johnson & Johnson, and Wal-Mart!

Google is barely 10 years old and it's bigger than Johnson and Johnson, which has been in business for over 120 years, or Walmart, which has been around for over 40 years.

To get a perspective on how large the Internet titans are, we can compare their annual revenues to the annual Gross Domestic Product of entire countries!

Thus, Apple's revenue is equal to all domestic production of Ecuador; Amazon is comparable to Kenya, Yahoo to Mongolia, and Microsoft to Croatia. Isn't that something…???

Google is facing competition for search from Amazon and aggregators such as Yelp, Manta, and wow.com.

It's still hard to find good information on Google, despite all the progress.

Yelp, for example does a much better job listing local restaurants on smartphones. If I'm looking for a breakfast place in a new town during a business trip, I won't use Google search to find the right place. Yelp has a superior interface, shows me the distance to a restaurant, and gives me a quick idea of its quality.

The same goes for Manta, when I do research for B2B companies.

The number of searches for products on Amazon exceeds the number of searches for the same products on Google by a factor of 3.

So, Google is not the only game in town...

- Facebook, Amazon, LinkedIn, and Pinterest all offer paid ads.
- Amazon will be facing a profitable Alibaba.

Nothing is certain in these fast changing tech industries, and the market dominance of top players cannot be taken for granted. We would not dare to predict how this market would look in just 5 years.

- Facebook has the largest number of users on mobile devices. This includes Instagram and WhatsApp.
- Mobile advertising is growing fast.
- Google, Apple, and Microsoft have their own browsers.
- Google controls Android – the operating system for the majority of smartphones in the world.

Globally, Google has a 63% market share in Search on desktops, and 92% on mobile devices.

In summary,

- Apple, Google, Facebook, Microsoft, and Amazon are here to stay
- Social media will see fads come and go as the younger generation will become ashamed of using Facebook, and Facebook will be buying up faddish new platforms as they did with Instagram and WhatsApp.
- The two mobile operating systems -- Android and iOS -- will dominate for years to come, with Android taking more market share.

- The titans are also getting into *The Internet of Things* space: Apple with iWatch and iBeacon and Google with the Nest thermostat

The Internet of Things, or the proliferation of cheap sensors in medicine, manufacturing, and construction, to name a few, combined with the ability to analyze data in real time, may bring about a powerful new player, as potential in this market is huge.

3.5

RECENT TRENDS

In the last section of the "Foundations" chapter, we'll cover the latest trends.

We already talked about it, but it's very important -- so let's repeat that over half of all searches today begin on smartphones, and 65% of emails are opened on smartphones. These numbers will only grow, and they have great impact -- especially on local B2C businesses that must have a good mobile presence, or they'll miss a lot of traffic.

There is definitely a trend toward using more video. Pages with videos convert better as they convey the message much better than text or static images. Video creation is still expensive and time consuming, but it's getting cheaper. A simple recorded slide presentation can make a great video, and it doesn't have to be produced by a top movie studio.

Another indisputable trend is toward much better content. Why is everyone talking about better content? There are several reasons:

- First of all, relevance – the more relevant content is to our search, the more likely visitors will engage and not leave our website immediately
- The better the copy, pictures, and video, the more likely visitors will engage

- And the better the content, the more likely the website will rank high in searches, because search engines have a way of evaluating content

Search engines will be rewarding quality because it's in their best interest. They don't want to produce listings with irrelevant and poor content because users will switch to the engine that does a better job of filtering out poor quality.

There is still a lot of work ahead of us, as the majority of websites don't do a good job of conveying the value proposition of their businesses.

Samsung's smartphone sales over the 2014 holidays were somewhere between 71 million and 75 million units— putting it roughly on par with Apple, which sold a record 74.5 million iPhones over the same period.

In general, it's expected that Android phones will outsell Apple, as various phone manufacturers can take advantage of the free Android operating system as opposed to the closely held Apple iOS.

Despite all the publicity, e-commerce in the U.S. accounts for less than 10% of sales in terms of revenue. Yes, a lot of people do shop online, but they buy small products while trying to avoid shipping costs. Thus, the average online transaction is rather small compared to brick-and-mortar retail transactions.

Despite being on the market for quite sometime, and despite the domination of e-commerce in the U.S., Amazon is not making a lot of money from e-commerce.

In general, e-commerce will experience downward pressures on profitability as the two titans fight things out. Unless you have a unique product, it will become harder to make decent margins on e-commerce, especially since Amazon tends to compete with its own suppliers.

As if digital marketing analysis was not very complex already, there's another analytical challenge facing B2C firms.

Due to the proliferation of smartphones, a lot of searches, price comparisons, and online purchases are taking place… *inside* stores.

It gets even more complicated as buyers search on multiple devices over periods of time, and then respond to last minute offers while they're still in the store. If they opt in to be tracked in the store, they may receive a coupon based on their location in the store and/or previous search patterns.

In such circumstances, it's hard to attribute any particular promotion to the actual sale.

These multi-channel buying journeys are here to stay, and in-store tracking is just taking off; so it remains to be seen how soon there will be a reliable way to keep track of such complex behaviors.

Big changes are coming to TV advertising as well.

It's predicted that by 2018, Internet advertising will be poised to overtake TV as the largest advertising segment. That means a big loss of revenue to traditional TV, which will only accelerate its demise in its current form.

Watching habits are changing, too. People are shifting to streaming services with clickable ads like Pluto TV. Or they subscribe to Netflix for $8 a month and drop cable subscriptions costing $150 per month.

Streaming TV has another great advantage over traditional TV. The ads are clickable and thus traceable. This is a huge advantage over traditional TV advertising where it's impossible to attribute the sale to an ad.

As we discussed previously, YouTube is already in the news and entertainment business. According to Nielsen, YouTube reaches more U.S. adults aged 18 to 34 than any cable network. And the younger generation doesn't need a big flat panel TV – they stream it on smartphones, tablets, and desktops.

We mentioned briefly before that Google is facing competition from aggregators with reviews.

Since Google does not specialize in any industry or search segment, it's hard to come up with relevant content, since the intentions of users are unknown.

Let me give you an example. If you search on the word 'coffee', Google has no way of knowing your intention. Is it to learn about coffee origins? Or to find the nearest coffee shop? So when you type 'coffee' into Google, you will get a lot of articles *about* coffee, while you may just be thirsty for a cup of coffee. If you type 'coffee' into Yelp, it will produce a list of coffee shops nearby, sorted by distance from your current location.

The same holds true for the word 'printer'. It has at least 3 meanings. Printer is a piece of hardware; it could be a print shop, or maybe a profession. So if I go to Manta, which aggregates information on businesses, and type 'printer', I know I will get a list of print shops as opposed to a list of ads for color laser printers.

That lack of knowledge of intent is hurting search engines. They still list a lot of irrelevant results and create a lot of frustration.

To make things even more challenging, **16% to 20% of queries that get asked every day** *have never been asked before.*

This is because the language is changing, and *how* questions are asked is changing. This is especially true for voice searches while driving.

As we said before, people search differently with voice on phones as compared to typing on desktops.

And speaking of smartphones…. In addition to searches and price comparisons, pretty soon we'll be making mobile payments. Whoever dominates mobile payments will make a lot of money. The importance of mobile presence and payments is demonstrated by these two examples.

- First, Home Depot has announced it will spend $1.5 billion to improve its supply chain and other back-end systems related to mobile ordering. This is a lot of money to make sure that customers can buy things with few clicks on their iPhone.

- Another example is Hilton Worldwide, which is investing $550 million to serve its guests in their 'mobile moments' and transform its entire customer experience.

3.6

RECENT TRENDS CONCLUSIONS

To summarize, we do *not* anticipate that the rate of technological change will slow down. If anything, it will accelerate.

There is a definite need to pay more attention to mobile presence, mobile advertising, videos, and streaming.

Creativity and innovation will become even more important. With so many technical alternatives, channels, and ways to communicate with customers, it will take a creative mind to pull it all together.

Very few individuals or even teams will have the skill sets to combine the creative, technical, and analytical aspects of digital marketing.

Few companies, especially smaller ones, will be able to attract and retain digital marketing talent. This leads me to believe that they will have to rely on a **network of specialized suppliers**.

There will be much more tracking and much more data to collect, store, and analyze. We'll be tracking more data, such as:
- Ad performance
- Search patterns
- Time spent watching video
- Opened email
- Social reach, Facebook likes, tweets, and re-tweets

- We'll track all this on multiple Internet channels

And

- o In stores
- o At home
- o While driving

After we collect all this data, someone will have to make sense of it. There will be a need for a lot of data analysis for optimal allocation of resources.

In general, we see a growing demand for multi-disciplinary talents like:

- Copywriters and copy editors
- Multimedia skills, especially video and voice talents
- Business analysts, marketing specialists and IT go-betweens
- Data analysis for drawing conclusions and recommending actions

As the famous Greek philosopher Heraclitus observed many years ago: "The Only Thing That Is Constant Is Change. "

Yes, there will be a lot of changes. We just have to learn how to manage them.

Digital marketing could be a ride in the fast lane. The roller coaster analogy is perfect here. There will be a lot of ups and downs, and it will be a team ride. It could be a little scary, but it promises a happy ending.

The likelihood of that happy ending increases with adherence to the best processes and practices of digital marketing.

And this is what we're going to discuss in the remaining chapters of our training.

So far, while discussing the Foundations of digital marketing, we covered the driving force behind all this rapid change. That driving force is less-expensive and more-powerful hardware and software.

We introduced the major players – fascinating new Internet businesses that made it to the top in less than 10 years, like Google, Facebook, Amazon.

Lastly, we looked at the latest Internet trends, with the most profound being the shift to mobile devices.

Next, we'll introduce our Digital Marketing Framework.

4.0

DIGITAL MARKETING FRAMEWORK

In the previous chapter, Foundations, we covered:

- Driving forces
- Major Internet players
- The most recent trends.

Now we're going to cover the 5 key channels of digital marketing, and we'll discuss how they work with each other to achieve maximum synergy to increase revenues and profits.

The Internet Marketing Framework is made up of marketing channels anchored by your website.

These channels are:

- Search
- Paid Ads
- Email
- Social media, and
- Traditional marketing

Search is about *how to be found* on the Internet. Search Engine Optimization, or SEO, is the set of techniques and processes to assure that your products and services are easily found by search engines such as Google, Yahoo, and Bing.

Paid ads is the marketing channel whereby you let the world know about your products by buying ads on Google, Facebook, and other social media, as well as applications, games, and so on.

Email is one of the under-appreciated assets of digital marketing. It's a major channel and it plays a crucial role, but it doesn't get as much publicity as SEO and social media.

Social Media gets a lot of attention and it's very important in B2C marketing; however, it has limited value in B2B marketing.

With the exception of pure-play Internet businesses such as e-commerce or games and apps on iTunes or in the Google store, digital marketing is supposed to work with and support **traditional marketing**.

Print, TV, and radio ads will be with us for quite some time. Their share is diminishing, but they are still effective marketing channels for many businesses.

Direct salespeople will always be with us, especially in B2B, where products or services are complex and require consultative selling.

Trade shows and old-time networking and relationship building on golf courses are not going away any time soon either. At the end of the day, people want to buy from people they like.

The heart of your Internet presence is your website, which "glues" all the channels together with common and consistent content.

That includes both look-and-feel (such as logos, fonts, and colors) as well as consistent message, copy, and keywords on all channels. Look-and-feel is relatively easy to keep consistent. It's much harder to have a consistent message with common keywords, especially in larger companies where multiple professionals are responsible for various channels.

The objective for all channels is to build and support your brand. In addition, the Internet Marketing Framework is responsible:

- In B2B, for providing qualified leads to the sales force
- In B2C, for driving physical traffic to 'brick and mortar' stores and increasing retail sales
- In E-commerce, for driving Internet traffic and converting it to sales online
- In politics, it's responsible for driving voters to polls

Our Internet Marketing Framework is both a logical model and a resource allocation model:

- As a Logical model, each channel has very well defined marketing roles, such as pulling the information in or pushing it out.
- As a Resource allocation model, it helps decide how to allocate resources, whether I have $1000 or $100 Million.

Each channel requires different skills and resources managed by various professionals (both internal and external). Each channel needs to be analyzed for its effectiveness and profitability, so both expenses and profits should be tracked by channel.

Last but not least, it's a great internal communication tool.

- Educates everyone on confusing digital marketing terminology
- Helps to communicate effectively to get consensus
- Illustrates digital marketing budget allocations, such as how much we're spending on email vs. SEO vs. paid ads

4.1

THE IMPORTANCE OF A WEBSITE

Let's now talk in more detail about the single most important component of our Framework. As you've probably guessed, it's your *website.*

- Your website is the heart of your **Internet presence.** The website offers equal opportunity to impress. Even a small business can afford a top-of-the-line site today. Websites are democratizing the Internet. A one-man shop business may look as good as a Fortune 500 company.

- Your website is the heart of your **marketing and sales.** It should be your Internet ambassador. It's often the first impression of your business.

- The heart of your **customer service**

    o   Maintaining, servicing, and up selling existing customers is a best business practice and the least expensive way to grow a business.

    o   Ask yourself this question: How much time is your sales force spending on service questions that could be been handled via your website? Paying high-earning sales people to answer simple questions about order status, shipments, product characteristics, etcetera, is not making them very effective.

You should make every effort to have your customers serviced online with as few clicks as possible.

Every website should build a **brand,** provide **sales leads or** generate **revenue,** and **service customers.**

In reality, most sites today are passive electronic business cards, just sitting pretty and contributing next to nothing to the bottom line.

- Your website needs to show well on smartphones, tablets, and desktops. Most still do not. This is very important, given the amount of Internet traffic generated on smartphones.
- It must load fast. Unfortunately, most businesses today don't know or track the loading speeds of their own sites.
- Easy navigation is of paramount importance.
- And it should not be built by your nephew or niece. ☺

You should make every reasonable effort to minimize the number of clicks for your visitors so they can get what they came for with minimum effort.

In general, you should use the rule of 5 clicks. Can your visitors get to your offer in 5 clicks or less? The average attention span of Internet visitors is just a few seconds.

Complex, hard to navigate websites are not only expensive to build and test; they also minimize the chances for conversions. Yes, you may be able to attract visitors to your website; but if they get frustrated with poor navigation after landing on it, your conversions will suffer a lot.

Sam Walton, the Wal-Mart founder (*if he were alive he would be the richest person in the world – his fortune got split between several family members*) has famously said:

"There is only one boss. The customer. And he can fire everybody in the company from the chairman on down, simply by spending his money somewhere else."

His comments are even more relevant on the Internet where the competition is just a click away! So please, remember, keep it simple!

Complexity is very expensive.

- A blog is a journal attached to your website
- It can be standalone if you are in the business of publishing. Huffington Post, for example, is technically a blog.
- Google expects sites to be updated at least once a month. A blog is the best way to accomplish that.
- Blogs are used to educate your prospects, customers, and employees.
- The best way to update a website is to post to a blog periodically, using the relevant keywords.
- Your blog can get you ranked in Google.
- But who writes it…?

A lot of businesses are frustrated with having to maintain blogs. After all, if you are a plumber, how much can you say about plumbing? In addition, most business owners aren't copywriters and aren't interested in writing.

Nevertheless, current SEO rules reward blogging. Copywriting services can be contracted out, and there are a lot of freelancers with blog writing skills. And don't forget proofreading or copyediting! Visitors can be turned off by sloppy text. Be sure everything you publish has been carefully screened for grammar and spelling to maintain high confidence in your company.

4.2

WEBSITE DESIGN CASE STUDY

Next, we'll walk you through a case study on website design. It will demonstrate best practices in designing and implementing a good revenue-generating website.

There are 4 Key Players in Website Creation. The first is the **Programmer,** who writes the software code. Typically a software engineer, they implement designs created by an architect.

The second is the **Graphic Designer.** Usually it's a Photoshop expert with a visual arts degree and some experience. They create a consistent graphical user interface that includes:
- Menus
- Fonts
- Layout and colors
- Photos

The Graphic Designer implements designs created by an architect.

The third is **Copywriter,** who writes the text. Typically it's an English major. They have the ability to write the brand story, and they are most effective when they understand the brand's positioning, the target audience, and their motivations.

The fourth is **the Architect,** who knows the business, knows SEO, and knows what is technically feasible. The Architect coordinates programmers, designers, and copywriters; provides briefs to copywriters; and creates wireframes for programmers and designers to function effectively.

Wireframes are very useful as a mock-up tool for designing websites. Like computerized sketching on a whiteboard, they allow us to prototype before locking down the design, and they are great for sharing the final design before coding.

Wireframes can be done in PowerPoint, however there are special software to do these mockups.

Briefs are detailed specifications for programmers and graphic designers. They're used to bid the work out.

Just as war is too important to leave to the generals, Website development is too important to leave to the technicians and graphic designers.

Or, for that matter, to your niece or nephew. ☺

The benefits of hiring an architect are threefold:

- The work gets done *right,* the first time
- Costs are minimized
- Time is saved

Without such specifications and briefs there is a lot of re-work a lot of guessing and it's very hard to get the right requirements from the users the first time.

Ask yourself a question:

Would you build your house without using an architect?

Your website is your single most important digital marketing asset!

As a reference, take a look at these websites:

www.conconow.com
www.itransact.com
www.rabin.com

They're excellent examples of rich content, easy navigation, a wealth of information, and they're also optimized for search engines and they represent large international and national American companies.

4.3

SEO INTRODUCTION

Now it's time to discuss the most complex digital marketing channel called SEO or Search Engine Optimization.

Do you remember the first rule of Digital Marketing? It was to "Find and to be Found".

This rule represents two sides of the same coin. On one hand you as a user, want to find what you are looking for very quickly among billions of websites. So you use search engine such as Google, Yahoo and Bing. You type what you're looking for and in the matter of seconds you get your answer.

On the other hand you want to be found as a business when a prospective client looks for a prospective supplier. Don't you? So as yourself a question: How important is it to your business to be easily found? What can you do to assure you can be found in seconds?

This channel is responsible for our products and services being found in a global digital haystack.

We'll cover the concepts and techniques to make sure that your website is catching all the buying signals from people who may be looking for your products and services worldwide.

The primary goal of SEO is to achieve the number one ranking on the first page of unpaid, organic results. It looks like FedEx did a good job being listed number one just below paid ads for the phrase "printing services" in Jacksonville, Florida.

In less technical terms, SEO means to make yourself findable by Google, Bing, and Yahoo when people search on the Internet for things you sell or…

…making sure that your prospective clients can find you on the Internet or…

… making sure your website "catches all the buying signals" from the Internet

Everybody wants to be #1 on Google.

Like a well-tuned radio antenna that catches all the radio signals from the air your website should be catching all the buying signals from the World Wide Web.

4.4

SEO DEFINITION

Let's discuss SEO definition

- SEO – Search Engine Optimization
- Optimization means editing your web pages to comply with search engine rules
- Optimization also involves link building

SEO is the process made of three steps:

1. Keyword selection
2. On-page optimization
3. Off-page optimization also referred to as a 'link building'

Keyword selection is about selecting keywords that your potential customers are likely to use while searching for products you sell.

We use Google Keyword Planner to find these keywords.

Step number 2 is on-page optimization is about placing selected keywords on your web pages according to Google 12 rules. For example, the keywords must be placed in page names, titles, headers, picture description, etc. The more rules your page complies with, the higher probability for high ranking

Step number 3 is about link building and it's about getting as many good quality links from other websites pointing to your website. This is a way for Google to evaluate the popularity of your website.

4.5

SEO - HOW IT WORKS

You may ask yourself a question: What does it take to be number 1? Your web page has to have relevant content that matches the keywords typed in the search box. This is accomplished by selecting the right keywords and putting them at the right places on your web pages.

You web page also has to be popular. Popularity is determined by the number of quality links or other websites pointing/linking to your website.

Let's see how SEO works.

Let's say I want to get new business cards printed somewhere near my office. I bring up Google in my browser and start my search by typing the word 'printing.'

Google doesn't know my intentions, but it tries to guess and suggests several options highlighted in bold. I decide on selecting "printing services." From my IP address, Google knows that I am in Jacksonville, Florida.

It is very important to understand the two key points:

1. Google stores all search phrases (keywords) that have ever been typed in by anyone who has ever done a search in Google.

This is made possible by technological advances that we talked about before.

2.   Google does not tell people how to search it just uses what you typed in and matches it with the content of websites.

This vast database of all searches provides powerful statistics on what is frequently being searched for. It is also used to provide suggestions for most popular related searches.

On one hand Google stores all the search phrases ever typed in, on the other hand Google software crawls the Internet and visits every web page from time to time.
Google stores the key components of these pages in its own databases, such as website name (url), page titles, headers, picture descriptions and much more. It can also store the name and physical address of your business.

This process is called indexing and it's a foundation how search engines work.

When I type in "printing services" Google will fetch all websites in Jacksonville (they know where I reside from my IP address). Then it will quickly look up among these website for any website that uses "printing services" as a keyword. Next it will present results ranked based on popularity of all the matching websites.

After I select or type in "printing services," Google presents me with a SERP – a Search Engine Results Page –with my search results in the form of a list of websites.

There are two types of listings: AdWords and organic. AdWords is the name of a Google program used to manage the creation and display of these ads.

Owners of these websites had to *pay* Google to show up on the first page of listings. The moment they stop paying, the ad disappears.

The ads position is based on a live auction among interested parties, and whoever pays the most gets listed at the top. We'll discuss this mechanism in more detail later in our book.

The listings that appeared in the bottom showed up there organically or naturally, based on the properties of these websites. Owners of these sites made a lot of effort to appear there – they followed all the SEO rules we'll be discussing soon.

Why is it so important to rank as high as possible?

Position on Google search page	Average % of clicks
1	22.23
2	10.22
3	7.00
4	5.05
5	3.60
6	3.45
7	3.15
8	2.39
9	2.18
10	2.06
Total	61.33

The above table makes it very easy to understand. The first organic position gets clicked by over 20% of people who search for printing services. The number 10 position gets one-tenth the number of clicks.

Why? Just because we're all very busy, we have short attention spans, and we don't want to scroll down if we don't have to.

So, this is a matter of simple math. The higher your listing appears or the higher your rank on the organic page, the more visitors you'll get.

No wonder that Tony Soprano, a violent gangster from HBO's The Sopranos series, smugly remarked that "The best place to hide a dead body is on the **second** page of Google."

It's very important to keep in mind that a high ranking is essential – but not sufficient in itself to get online leads.

Your listing has to be enticing and relevant so people will want to click on it.

Once they're on your site, they better find what they're looking for or they'll leave immediately.

Remember our golden rule of digital marketing? We need to attract, bring, and convert. SEO just deals with attracting visitors. If the other parts are not in place, investment in SEO will not produce much in the way of results.

Let's look at two listings from the top page for keyword "printing services".

Inky Fingers Jacksonville Printing Company – Inky Fingers… www.inkyfingers.biz
Inky Fingers is a full service Jacksonville printer with 4-color process printing and full bindery capabilities, serving clients nationwide.

Custom Printing Services – Copy & Print Depot
www.officedeopt.com

Custom printing services at Copy & Print Depot deliver everything from business cards to promotional products. Same day printing and pickup is available.

Both companies did a great job of getting listed on the first page, but Office Depot did much better bringing me to their site.

Inky Fingers repeated their name 3 times in the listing, wasting a lot of characters. I probably don't care what the name of the printing shop is at this point, and I probably don't care that they have 4-color process printing and full bindery capabilities. I just want to get my business cards printed.

Office Depot, on the other hand, informed me that they do business cards and they have same-day printing and pick-up.

We have a clear winner here!

4.6

SEO CASE STUDY - COMMERCIAL PRINTING

I want to share with you a case study that provides even more insides into the concepts that we've already discussed. I'll present it based on our experience with a 20 million dollar commercial printing company.

To illustrate this very important concept, we'll use a commercial printing company case.

We'll use our familiar 3-step SEO process to provide the context to this case.

A reminder, the 3-step process consists of:

1. Keyword selection
2. On-page optimization
3. Off-page optimization, also called link building

Step number 1, keywords selection is made of three phases:

1. Keyword research

2. Keyword evaluation based on importance, relevance and competition
3. Keyword selection based on combination of
   a. Highest importance
   b. Most relevance
   c. Lowest competition

Keywords search and selection is the single most important component of any successful SEO effort. In real estate it's location, location, location. In SEO it's keywords, keywords, keywords. If you get this part wrong, it's impossible to get the rest of the process right.

During the Research phase we need to learn how potential customer may be looking for our products and services on the Internet. For this purpose we use Google Keyword Planner – a free tool for keyword search.

To illustrate this very important concept, I'll use a commercial printer company

Here is the description of their services on their website:

"We specialize in Corporate Communications • Magazines • Catalogs • Presentation Folders • Direct Mail • Fulfillment Services • Packaging & Labeling • Sales & Marketing Materials • Brand Identity Items • Training Materials • Graphic Design • Sheet-fed Offset Printing • Heat-set Web Printing • UV & Aqueous Coatings • Foil Stamping • Embossing • Die Cutting • Custom printed tuck end auto bottom boxes • Saddle Stitching • Perfect Binding • Inkjet Addressing • Poly Bagging • Mailing"

And here are the most popular searches on Google typed in when people are looking for printing services:

Keywords	Monthly Searches
printers	6,600
brochure	4,400
screen printing	4,400
printing services	3,600
flyer	3,600
print	2,900
printing	2,400
poster printing	1,600
brochures	1,300
sticker printing	1,000
label printer	880
online printing	880
bookbinders	880

This was done using Keyword Planner. It turned out that the word "printers" was typed into Google 6,600 times in the last month in the United States.

Look at this side-by-side comparison of how this printing company describes itself versus how people look for their printing services.

Keywords used when searching	Keywords used on the website
printers	Corporate communication
brochure	magazines
screen printing	catalogs
printing services	Presentation folders
flyer	Direct mail
print	Fulfillment services
printing	Packaging & labeling
poster printing	Sales & marketing materials
brochures	Brand identity items
sticker printing	Training materials
label printer	Graphic design
online printing	Sheet-fed offset printing
bookbinders	Heat-set web printing

Do you see even one match between these two tables?

This site has zero chances of being found when people are looking for printing services -- unless they incorporate some of the terms people use to perform searches.

If you understand this concept, you understand the spirit of SEO.
It's about what your customers want to see -- not what you want to show off!

The description of your products and services on your website MUST match the keywords used to search for them.

Think about how potential customers may be looking for you.

If I want to order business cards, do I really care about how you print them?

Next you have to evaluate keywords for importance.

Importance is directly tied to the number of searches for it. The more searches the keyword has had, the more visits it will generate.

We create a list of keywords we select using the *Keyword Planner* tool, and we put them in a spreadsheet and sort high to low.

The top keyword "printers" has a lot of searches, but it may include searches for hardware such as inkjet printers or printing services.

Each keyword needs to be evaluated for relevance.

In our example here, what is more relevant to my business? If I specialize in printing brochures and my website content reflects that, I may want to emphasize this keyword as opposed to the more generic "printing services."

I may get more visits with "printing services," but fewer people will convert as many of them may not be looking for *brochure* printing.

On the other hand, if someone searches for a "brochure" and they land on my website devoted to brochure printing, I have higher chances of converting this traffic to actual business.

Using specialized tools, we can evaluate each keyword for its competition.

Using a specialized tool such as **Market Samurai**, we can find the top ranking sites for keyword *brochure*. The analysis will reveal if the keyword "brochure" is being used in page titles, URLs, descriptions, and headers.

We may find out, for example that, 9 out of 10 of our competitors already use "brochure" in the important parts of their web pages – the part that Google is looking at and where it does its matching.

In a nutshell, such analysis shows us that there is a lot of competition on the Internet for keyword "brochure"

Thus, we may not have a choice – we have to balance high relevance with low competition.

Remember, we're trying to get ranked on many keywords, so if we don't rank on some, it's not the end of the world. We need to come up with a combination of high relevance keywords with better chances for ranking. This is an art, not a science.

The next step is on-page optimization.

On-page optimization is a fancy term referring to the way you need to use keywords on your website and web pages

You need to use keywords in several places on your website. The keywords must be correctly placed in:

- Copy
- Directory names
- Page titles
- Headers
- Descriptions
- Photo descriptions
- Menus
- ….and many more

Google publishes their rules and the more you adhere to them, the better chances for rankings.

Page optimization can get results in terms of weeks. Nevertheless, it may take up to 6 month to reach the optimal ranking. Maintaining such ranking will require constant watching what competition is doing, link building and adding relevant content.

Let's discuss off-page optimization, also referred to as link building.

As we mentioned before, Google rewards relevance and popularity.

Popularity is created by off-page optimization or link building.

You need to:

- Get links to your website – quantity
- Assure that relevant/strong domains link to your website – quality
- Links from .edu, .gov or NYT have much more weight that links from your friends

Link building is very time consuming. The value of link building increases with the competition for keywords.

If two competing pages have identical on-page optimization, the one what will rank higher will be the one with more links to it.

Link building is about promoting your website

To do such promotion well you should:

- Write a blog on your website
- Guest blog on friendly websites
- Get customer review published on the third party review sites
- Comment on social media
- Claim directory listings
- Pick up a phone and ask for a link

You need to make sure that the promoted content contains links to pages you're trying to promote. Google will crawl and count your links. It's about quantity with quality

Link building requires an ongoing effort, keeping your site fresh. It calls for the regular creation of posts and blogs.

It's a challenge for a lot of businesses that, in the past, did not have to worry about such mundane activities. Such services can be outsourced to experienced copywriters

4.7

SEO OTHER CASE STUDIES

To conclude the section on SEO I'd like to introduce additional Case Studies.

The first case study presents an ecommerce, B2C, business-to-consumer company, that does business nationwide. The average profit per sale transaction is $5.00.

The second case study is a global B2B website with very few visitors and conversions, but very large transactions. Average profit per transaction is about $100K.

In order to make profit the ecommerce company needs a lot of visits, a lot of conversions and needs a lot of transactions and sales.

The traditional website with a very large average transaction requires few visits, few conversions and one transaction can pay for the cost of the SEO project.

Let's explore the case study about ecommerce B2C company with lots of small transactions.

GREG GUTKOWSKI

The company is a large seller of specialty clothing online. It was only ranking for 7 non-branded keywords prior to the SEO program, and averaging about 3,000 visits per month from non-branded keywords.

This table shows their rankings at the beginning of the project and 1 year later.

Keyword	Keyword Monthly Search Volume	Google Rank at project start date	Google Rank 1 year later
Black leotards	1000		1
Dance competition costumes	1300		2
Ballet tights	720		3
Dance costumes for competition	5400		3
Hip hop dance costumes	1600	8	4
Bloch dancewear	1000		5
Leotards for girls	3600		5
Lyrical dance costumes	3600		5
Dance recital costumes	4400		6
Dance shoes online	1000	9	6
Jazz dance costumes	1600		6

Keyword	Keyword Monthly Search Volume	Google Rank at project start date	Google Rank 1 year later
Dance shorts	1600		8
Girls leotards	880		8
Discount leotards	720		9
Hip hop shoes	2400		9
Dance attire	1000		10
Discount dance wear	1000		10
Capezio shoes	1600		11
Dance clothing	2900	15	12
Dance wear	9900	10	12
Dance clothes	6600	12	14
Dance accessories	880	11	15
dancewear	27100	15	16

The third column shows the ranks for several non-branded keywords at the beginning of the project. The highest position was 8 for "hip hop dance costumes." Many keywords had not ranked at all.

The last column shows the ranks after 12 months of SEO efforts.

It looks like many of the keywords that didn't rank in the beginning are ranking now in positions from 1 to 10. This is great news!

However, notice that several keywords at the bottom of the table lost their ranks. Not a lot but nevertheless…

You may wonder why this happened. It looks like the keywords that slipped in ranks are more generic, and there is a growing competition for them. On the other hand, high rankings were achieved for more detailed and specific keywords. This is very typical for SEO – it's easier to get ranked for niche keywords as opposed to generic ones.

Google Analytics showing an increase in impressions from 10,000 to about 250,000 as a result of SEO efforts.

We'll discuss Google Analytics in more depth in the Analytics chapter of our book. For now, suffice it to say that Google Analytics is a free tool from Google that keeps track of every click *ever* on your website --in real time, online. It's invaluable in analyzing what works and what doesn't, as it can aggregate all the clicks over time and for various demographics. For example, we know how many times a page was visited, how long the visitor stayed there, where they clicked next, and what forms they filled out, to name a few.

With another Google tool called Search Console (used to be called Webmaster Tool) , we can track our link-building efforts by analyzing the number of links to each new page.

In this case, using Search Consoled we learned that links increased from 659 to 4,519! The more the better!

We can watch trends or clicks over time. Using this view of Google Analytics, we learned that in the last quarter, the traffic quadrupled as compared to the last year and prior to the start of our SEO project.

In the end, it's not about visits - it's about sales. Here again, with the help of online analytics, we were able to see that sales went up 256% when compared to pre-SEO time. Very impressive results indeed.

Let's switch to the other end of the SEO spectrum and look at a global B2B website with very few visitors and conversions, but very large transactions. Average profit per transaction is about $100K.

The traditional website with a very large average transaction requires few visits, few conversions and one transaction can pay for the cost of the SEO project.

This customer is a Global Asset Auction and Liquidation Service. They have offices in San Francisco, in the U.S., and in Manchester, UK. They assist huge corporations with the liquidation of machinery and equipment or entire plants as well as industrial and commercial real estate.

Similar to the first case, the customer did not rank at all on any of the relevant keywords shown in the following table.

The table shows 6 months of progress in ranking of various keywords. The company ranked on no keywords at all in May when the SEO project started. 6 months of SEO resulted in:

- 13 First page rankings (position of 10 or less)
- 12 Second page rankings
- 3 Third page rankings

And they started getting leads.

Just one such lead can result in a multimillion-dollar transaction!

In summary, I've shown you two different SEO test cases. One requires a lot of visits and conversions and the average transaction is quite low. The other one is a B2B company where just a few leads can pay for the project many times over. This is why I believe that B2B organizations with a large average transaction have a tremendous potential to increase their business with very little expense.

Keyword	Monthly Searches	Baseline ranking May	July	June	Aug	Sept	Oct	Nov
Asset recovery	2400	-	-	-	-	-	-	-
Company liquidation	1600	-	-	-	-	-	-	28
Voluntary liquidation	1600	-	-	-	-	13	19	15
Asset valuation	1300	-	-	-	20	-	-	-
Asset sales	1000	-	-	-	-	-	-	-
Creditors voluntary liquidation	880	-	-	-	15	19	10	15
Machinery auctioneers	390	-	-	-	-	19	-	-
Liquidation companies	390	-	-	-	-	-	15	11
Commercial liquidators	320	-	18	-	20	11	12	12
Industrial liquidators	320	-	-	-	17	19	16	16
Asset recovery services	260	-	18	-	9	6	14	15
Liquidation services	210	-	-	-	7	8	6	15
Auction liquidation services	170	-	10	15	7	9	11	8
Asset liquidation	170	-	-	-	18	18	17	17
Voluntary liquidation process	170	-	-	-	-	-	17	9

Keyword	Monthly Searches	Baseline ranking May	July	June	Aug	Sept	Oct	Nov
Asset appraisal services	110		13	19	15	6	12	12
Asset appraisal	110	-	8	16	10	9	14	14
Convert assets into cash	70	-	11	19	7	7	7	6
Industrial appraisal	50	-	16	-	5	5	9	10
Creditors voluntary liquidation process	30	-	8	-	8	9	4	4
How to liquidate a limited company	30	-	8	-	3	3	3	3
Equipment appraisal services	30	-	18	-	18	19	10	4
What is voluntary liquidation of a limited company	10	-	-	-	4	4	4	4
Heavy equipment appraisal services	10	-	14	18	11	10	8	5
Asset liquidation process	<10	-	5	9	5	7	5	5
How to convert assets into cash	<10	-	9	-	8	2	3	1
Industrial appraisal services	<10	-	9	-	8	9	10	9
Machinery appraisal services	<10	-	9	17	7	6	8	17

4.8

SEO SUMMARY

To summarize our section on SEO I believe that SEO is the single most important investment in digital marketing that you can make.

I compare it to 'basic hygiene.' Like washing your hands is the cheapest way to avoid sickness, getting SEO right is the cheapest way to grow your business.

SEO is about catching all the buying signals from the Internet.

In summary, SEO is a digital asset to stay with you for years to come. It will bring recurring benefits, catching all the buying signals from the Internet.

And SEO is the 7/24/365 sales person who never sleeps, complains, or asks for a raise. ☺

SEO has a very high return on investment, especially when the average sale is large (over $50,000).

4.9

EMAIL MARKETING

In this section, we'll discuss email marketing one of the most underappreciated channels of digital marketing.

For some people, email is still associated with spam and scam. As a result of email spam, several countries have passed strict laws regarding unsolicited email.

For example, in the U.S., each business email solicitation must have a physical address of a company listed and provide an option to be removed from future emails.

However, email has been such an integral part of our lives that it's impossible to imagine how we were able to live without it.

For many individuals, myself included, an email address is one of the permanent ingredients of self-identification. For the last 15 years, I've had the same email address but 3 different street addresses (because I moved three times), 6 different phone numbers, and 3 different bank account numbers. So the only permanent parts of my identity were my name, date of birth, social security number, and email address.

Our email address is our de facto passport to the Internet. It's often used as a username for online services. Our email addresses are part of our identification, authentication, and verification.

Most services send us emails as a transaction confirmation, including receipts for purchases made in brick and mortar stores.

Email marketing shows high ROI when compared to other channels because it's inexpensive but impactful.

It used to be that if you wanted to illustrate a concept in an email, you had to attach a picture. Not anymore. The picture can be embedded in the body of an email without clogging email inboxes.

Technically speaking, when we open emails today, we're using the same technology as websites as far as fetching pictures and videos. So the body of your email can be populated with images, colors, and formatting that are rendered in real time, and you store nothing on your computer. Just like with regular browsing.

This technology allows for the creation of very rich email content—comparable to regular websites. Actually, one best practice of email marketing is to make the look and feel of your emails match your website. You've probably seen very nice email messages with beautiful pictures, embedded videos, and great graphics.

Thus, an email message is like sending a single website page to a smartphone.

There are several competing email services on the market. For a comparative analysis please visit this website:

https://www.g2crowd.com/categories/email-marketing-best-of-breed

The top packages are all very similar in capabilities. The differences between them are like those between Honda and Toyota – they all work very well. Sometimes it's just a matter of preference.

They're all based on the concept of using templates and lists for campaigns.

A campaign is referred to as a single mailing to a certain group or list of recipients using a certain message or template.

Lists can be tagged by known demographics such as age, gender, physical location, and so on. These tags can be used to create sub-lists, and campaigns can be mailed to any sub-list. Thus, one master list of all known email addresses can be used, reused, and managed in one place.

In addition, we can create a set of templates to be used and reused for various repetitive messages or campaigns. Imagine an e-commerce site that sends out two campaigns every winter – one for girls and one for boys outerwear—using the same sub-lists and templates with only minor modifications.

Due to that structure of templates, lists, and sub-lists, email marketing is very flexible, customizable, and made relevant with relatively little effort. Templates can be copied and modified, and sub-lists are maintained automatically; so a new campaign every year or month can be executed very quickly.

More sophisticated usage can be based on rule-based workflows. For example, think about sending a different email to someone who has purchased versus to someone who has just filled out a request for more information – two different templates will do the job.

Emails are great for prospecting if those prospects opt in. There are several techniques to entice folks into sharing their email addresses. They include giveaways, discounts, contests, coupons, and so on. In general, you should make the collection of good email addresses one of the foundations of your digital marketing strategy.

Emails are even more effective in keeping existing customers happy and engaged. If a customer is happy with you, they will more likely open emails from you. The more engaging the content of these emails, the more likely they will purchase more from you.

You should make every effort to communicate with your existing base in such a way that they don't perceive it as nuisance, but as information sharing.

Each email should have a forward-to-a-friend button as well as buttons for social media sharing to make it very easy for happy customers to spread the word for you.

Interestingly, social media uses email as a part of their engagement strategy. Facebook, Twitter, and LinkedIn all send emails about updates on status, published posts, possible new friends or followers, and so on.

They probably realize that you are more likely to check email before you visit their portals. This is probably the best testimonial to the power of email as a marketing channel.

Today emails are traceable, which makes them even more powerful marketing tools.

Let's say we sent our 1,000 emails. The email system will tell us how many were opened and by whom—the open rate,

How many opted out,

How many clicked on links in the email—the click rate,

And how many may have responded to calls for action, such as responding to a survey in the body of an email.

You also get a comparison of current open and click rates to previous campaigns and industry averages. That's a great way to measure your email effectiveness!

If your email contains links to your website where the email recipient purchases something, we can then trace a single communication to the actual sale – something that has never been possible or inexpensive in the past.

So you can compare campaigns not only on open or click rates, but also on actual sales!

Email programs are very easy to use; no programming skills are required.

They're inexpensive compared to snail mail.

And they're mobile friendly—which is very important when 65% of emails are opened on smartphones.

The popularity of email and our dependence on it may also be explained by the fact that our emails are used as:

- Filing cabinets,
- Follow-up reminders,
- Audit trails,
- Reference and documentation.

A lot of busy professionals prefer emails to phone calls, especially when synchronous interaction is not required.

Thus there's a good chance that one of your emails may get archived and then opened later as a result of an email search a year from now—maybe even leading to a big sale! ☺

Here are some email best practices:

- Keep it simple – both the title line and the message
- Don't mail more than once a month
- Do A/B testing on various subject lines and content

- Put links in email messages to relevant web pages to enhance your message and allow for analysis of which links have the most impact.
- Treat your email database like a strategic asset.

- Grow it every chance to you get
- Keep it clean
- And protect it– it has a lot of value!

"You've got an infinite number of emails!"

We are all challenged to manage a never-ending stream of emails...

On the other hand, I would be scared if I didn't get a single email one day! ☺

4.10

SOCIAL MEDIA INTRODUCTION

The next marketing channel we'll be going over is social media—the concept that took the world over in just the last 10 years.

It's a must to master for some types of businesses and has at least marginal value to some others. We'll discuss their differences and walk through the major players in this space.

There are so many social media platforms that it's hard to keep track of them all. But just like everything else in marketing, there is an 80/20 rule; that is, 20 percent of the players control 80 percent of the market.

This is also a market with some global players such as Facebook, Twitter, and LinkedIn as well as players limited only to their native markets in Russia, China, or South Korea.

Social media are sometimes referred to as "Weapons of Mass Distraction" due to the amount of trivia, gossip, and low-value content.

Nevertheless, it's a great invention and, if used wisely, it enriches the lives of so many people, especially geographically dispersed families and friends.

As for its value to digital marketing, the role of social media is very different in the news business, business to consumer (or B2C) companies, and B2B organizations.

In the news\entertainment\politics arena, they are crucial to branding, engagement, and buzz generation. You live and die by the mastery of Facebook and Twitter.

For B2C companies, social media are very important as well. This is especially true for any trendy, fashion-related products geared to a younger audience. In addition to social engagement, social media are now being used for customer service as well.

In B2B, social media are of much less value as a marketing channel. It's unlikely that a steel fabrication company is going to get leads from Facebook. In many B2B firms, direct sales people play a crucial role in growing the business. Listening to social media can provide them with high-value market and sales intelligence. We advise our B2B customers to set up a social media listening system before they invest a lot in their own social media activities. We'll discuss it in more detail later in the book.

Social media presence, if done right, is very time-consuming and very hard to directly attribute to an increase in sales. This is an expensive channel with fuzzy ROI.

Only 70 years ago, landowners in Eastern Europe were getting isolated from the real world every year for about 6 months. They lived on large estates with no roads passable to mail services due to snow starting about early November. Then until May, roads were too muddy. There was no radio, and the last delivery of newspapers and magazines was in November. For 5 or 6 months, there was no news about national or international events. The favorite pastime was betting on how the national and international events would unfold in the next half year. There was a lot of guessing and speculation. The true nature of events did not become known until May when the first newspapers finally reached their estates.

I think this must have been true in some parts of the U.S. and Canada as well, before radio was widespread.

So, in the space of not so many years in human history, we went from a 6-month drought on news to a deluge of trivia every waking moment of our lives. ☺

4.11

SOCIAL MEDIA OVERVIEW

This chart shows social media companies with over 100 million active users. The numbers are just staggering.

	Active Users in Millions
Facebook	2,070
YouTube	1,500
WhatsApp	600
Messenger	1,000
WeChat	963
Instagram	600
Skype	300
Twitter	328
LinkedIn	500

Facebook leads the pack with over 2 billion active users. This would have been unthinkable only 10 years ago! Nobody pays for membership. The whole model is based on cheap hardware and software supported by advertising.

Note that WhatsApp and Instagram are also Facebook properties, so Facebook's dominance as a company is unquestionable at this time.

YouTube is number 2 with over a 1.5 billion users.

There are several Chinese players, too, but their market is mostly limited to China. Skype, LinkedIn, and Twitter dwarf in comparison however. The importance of LinkedIn and Twitter in B2B digital marketing is not reflected in this chart, but it can't be overlooked.

Let's discuss common social media threads.

First, there's buzz and fads. A lot of social media were hijacked by the celebrity and gossip business where they are prone to Hollywood trends and fads. The social media themselves are subject to fads, with younger generations refusing to use Facebook because it's not 'cool' enough. So they switch to Instagram, which is, ironically, owned by Facebook.

Most likely there will always be new 'cool' entrants to this market that will be bought out by major players.

Sometimes social media fads remind me of the situation with music bands that fall out of style at the expense of the younger, more 'cool' kids.

In politics and B2C – ignore Facebook at your peril. Most recent U.S. elections were won by the party who leveraged social media to get out the vote.

If you are in a B2C business, especially fashion and other trendy items, you have to have a strong social media strategy and presence.

Social media form a growing competitive threat to news organizations. Twitter, Yahoo, Facebook, YouTube, and now Apple are investing heavily in displacing ABC, NBC, CBS, and the New York Times as a source for go-to news. We talked about the trend to streaming and away from cable in the Foundations chapter. Mainstream media so far have no viable answer to this trend.

Social media are all search engines by themselves, thus becoming competitors to Google search. The more people use them and the more content they have, the more valuable and relevant search results can be provided.

All social media are great for market research and intelligence. Twitter and Facebook 'fire hoses,' YouTube viewing patterns, and LinkedIn discussions provide unheard of amounts of data that can be harvested for marketing research and competitive analysis. We'll discuss this subject in more detail in the Competitive Analysis chapter.

Facebook, Twitter, and LinkedIn are the basis for social selling – the concept of using social media to prospect and to engage potential clients through social media. We will be discussing this concept in depth in the 'Digital Selling' section.

All social media welcome both company and private profiles. This brings about the important issue of communication policy for companies. Do we have a single voice? Who is responsible for the message? What is the approval process?
Last but not least, all social media players use email extensively to engage with their users.

Let's start our overview of key social media players with Facebook.

- As mentioned before, it's a must-have for B2C and politicians
- One in five page views in the United States occurs on Facebook[3]
- It provides precisely targeted ads based on age, interests, hobbies, and gender, to name a few

- Facebook supports business pages, too, and is great for brand building and reputation management.
- Facebook has been acquiring complementary and/or competitive services, including WhatsApp messaging and Instagram, which has the most active users
- It is fad sensitive – especially among the younger population who cares about the 'cool factor' and has turned their attention to Instagram to Facebook's benefit.
- The company offers an internal corporate version whereby all the functionality is available inside company and protected from outside interference.
- There are some Privacy concerns – Facebook is not known for great respect for it.
- And there are Censorship concerns – Facebook has terms of use that are not in line with the First Amendment. What is protected speech on the Federal level may be barred from Facebook. This is especially relevant to any partnership with news organizations such as the New York Times.

And now on to Twitter, the least understood in the business.

- It's a must-have for B2C
- All the so-called "opinion leaders" use it
- It forces concise communication – Twitter came into its own with texting and it has become a fierce competitor to news organizations
- Twitter is all about reputation management around both personal and company accounts or "handles"
- You may not need to tweet, but you should definitely listen in. We'll elaborate on the topic in the Competitive Analysis section of this book.

Twitter is even used by the CIA.

Here is their first tweet – and this is a real tweet:

"We can neither confirm nor deny that this is our first tweet."

The real challenge with Twitter is how to separate the relevant from billions of tweets – which we'll cover in the Competitive Analysis chapter.

Measuring impact with hashtags and keywords is a best practice.

- They are location specific and can track tweets from around a conference hall.
- Hashtags allow for live participation, for example, during conferences.

Twitter has overtaken LinkedIn as the Number 1 Social Media Site for Salespeople.

This is from May 2015. The amount of tweeting among C-level executives is on the rise, so it's no wonder that this is a great 'snooping' ground for sales folks.

The power of Twitter is related to the snowballing effect of the network.

A single tweet may reach 100 recipients almost instantly. What if you had a million followers?

Forget a million—how about 71 million, like Katy Perry?

You may think – I am not in news, politics, or the celebrity business. That's why we prepared this table for you.

	# of followers in million
Dalai Lama	17.4
CNN	54.2
The New York Times	41
Facebook	14
Muhammad Al-Arifi	20.9
Starbucks Coffee	11.9
Whole Foods Market	4.9
Donald Trump	47.1
Hillary Clinton	21.4

Note the number of followers for Whole Foods Market, and Starbucks Coffee. These staggering numbers are very helpful in spreading any promotional message. For the sake of comparison, we're showing followers for known politicians as well.

All tweets are in the public domain. There are software packages allowing users to 'listen' to all the relevant tweets by grouping them in different folders based on filters such as handles, hashtags, and keywords. Without such tools, Twitter is just not manageable; but with the right set-up, it can provide surprisingly good market intelligence. We'll cover these techniques in the Competitive Analysis chapter as well.

As for LinkedIn:

- It's a must-have for B2B sales professionals who use it for social selling

- And it's a must-have for recruiting & job search, talent, partner, and supplier search
- LinkedIn contains robust professional profiles, or living resumes, for both individuals and companies
- It also accommodates affinity groups and their discussions
- As a vast publishing platform, LinkedIn is a great place to take the pulse of issues and reactions.

LinkedIn is quite effective in B2B advertising. Like Facebook, LinkedIn allows for ads targeted to personal demographics based on job responsibilities, tenure, industries, and years of experience.

It also allows advertising to known email addresses only, thus avoiding a lot of wasteful gunshot advertising.

LinkedIn also has a little known feature that allows large companies to have sub-pages, called Showcase Pages, to feature separate product lines under one corporate umbrella. Microsoft, for instance, has taken full advantage of this feature.

Pinterest is a relative newcomer to social media. It arose from a brilliant idea allowing people to pin pictures of their hobbies to a virtual display board.

It's a must-have for B2C, especially product companies, targeting personal hobbies, interests, dreams, and aspirations. It also accommodates targeted ads, search, and personal and company profiles.
With the power of simplicity, Pinterest breeds affiliate programs launched by pretty pictures.

Last but not least is YouTube – the giant of videos. There is an indisputable trend toward video content and its growing importance in digital marketing. That's because 90% of information transmitted to the brain is visual, and visuals are processed 60,000 times faster in the brain than text.

We've seen that videos on landing pages increase average page conversion rates by 86%!

As an example of growing YouTube importance, the President of the U.S. gave the first presidential interview on YouTube in January 2015.

It's very strong competition to TV news and entertainment, online training, and learning. And they just hired a top MTV executive to lead its music business!

An individually owned channel is a convenient and low-cost way to manage and promote content.

Beware, though. As with all social media, censorship and copyright issues are still not resolved to everybody's satisfaction.

In summary, we wanted to share with you this clever depiction of the differences between various social media platforms. *Anonymous*

Social Media Explained ☺	
Twitter	I'm eating a #donut ☺
Facebook	I like donuts ☺
Foursquare	This is where I eat donuts ☺
Instagram	Here's a vintage photo of my donut ☺
YouTube	Here I am eating a donut ☺
LinkedIn	My skills include donut eating ☺
Pinterest	Here's a donut recipe ☺
LastFM	Now listening to "Donuts" ☺
G+	I'm a Google employee who eats donuts. ☺

4.12

PAID ADS INTRODUCTION

The final and equally important component of our Digital Marketing Framework is paid ads. After all, the revenue from these ads is the foundation of Google's wealth. In other words, revenue from online ads has financed the digital marketing industry.

We mentioned already that this unique business model was brought about due to very inexpensive technology. At one point, it became financially feasible for social media platforms to give away online services for free, build up a large following, and then start selling the ads.

Advertisers fell in love with online ads. They were cheaper, more effective, and allowed for precise tracking. For the first time in the history of the advertising industry, one could tie the cost of ads to the actual revenues.

That was almost impossible in the past with respect to print, radio, and TV advertising.

Phillip Morris used to spend millions on worldwide and world famous Marlboro advertising without knowing exactly where the diminishing returns occurred. Was $100 million enough? Or maybe we should spend $90, or maybe $120 million. No one really knew – these decisions were made on gut and experience.

So from the financial and measurement perspective, they were shooting from the hip.

As an advertising pioneer, John Wanamaker stated, "Half the money I spend on advertising is wasted; the trouble is I don't know which half."

Clickable online ads solved this problem forever.

The Measurement Revolution we've talked about is all about shooting from hip. Now we know:

- How many times the digital ad was displayed to whom
- How many people clicked on it
- How many people called and/or filled out a form
- How much actual revenue could be attributed to a specific ad

This is how the Measurement Revolution was born.

Next let's discuss the 3 types of paid online ads. They include:

- Search
- Display
- Remarketing

4.13

PAID SEARCH ADS

Let's start with **paid search ads**, also referred to as **Google ads**, or **AdWords ads**.

When a user types a search term or keyword into Google, a list of results shows up.

Organic listings display just below the top 3 listings. We did **not** have to pay Google to show up there, but we **did** have to follow Google SEO guidelines to get there.

Advertisers who sell red shoes log into Google AdWords, which is a Google platform to create, manage and buy ads.

In AdWords, they write a short listing that will show up when users search for red shoes, for example. Here we have two examples of such listings from JC Penney and Kohl's.

As a part of ad setup advertisers tell AdWords how much they want to spend when a user clicks on their listing. If the user doesn't click, there is no payment.

In simple terms, if JC Penney is willing to pay even one cent more than Kohl's, their ad will show ahead of Kohl's.

Without going into a lot of detail, there is a real time auction among many red shoes sellers, and there are some complex algorithms helping to optimize the advertising budgets. The seller has control over when the ad should appear and where. Thus, for example, you can show your ads only on weekends to selected zip codes.

This concept makes for very efficient advertising and explains why advertisers love it—subject to prices, of course!

If a user clicks on your red shoes ad and subsequently buys the shoes online, you'll have a very clear picture of how effective such an advertisement was.

As mentioned before the advertiser pays only for clicks—hence the name **Pay-Per-Click** for this advertising model.

As mentioned before, it is based on real time auction, and advertisers have a lot of flexibility in the timing and location of their ads.

This model is the basis for over 90% of Google's revenues. Google dominates this industry with a very high market share.

Bing and Yahoo together have remaining 25% of the market share.

Pay per click seems like a simple concept, but it's very easy to get it wrong—and still pay Google! ☺

Let's first start with a good example.

I'm looking for a wedding photographer in Jacksonville, Florida.

I will type "wedding photographer Jacksonville, fl' in a search box

The following SERP, or ad, shows up and catches my attention:

Wedding Photographer $650

www.photopage/com/weeedings
Quality Photography A Promise
Your Jacksonville Wedding

This ad confirms that this is about a wedding photographer in Jacksonville.

When I click on it and I see a beautiful wedding picture. I like the sample. I pick up the phone and call this photo shop to make an appointment.

Remember the golden rule of ABC of digital marketing? A for attract, B for bringing and C for converting. This photography studio did a great job attracting, bringing and converting me to become their customer.

In summary, I found what I was looking for very quickly and the photographer paid just a couple of dollars for a new customer.

We have a win-win scenario here.

Let's examine a PPC case where things went wrong

In this example, I'm looking to go deep see fishing in Jacksonville. (By the way, Jacksonville is located right on the shores of the Atlantic Ocean.)

I type "deep see fishing in Jacksonville FL"

The following SERP, or ad, shows up

Florida Deep Sea Fishing

www.fishtaxicharters.com
Guaranteed Fish – Reserve Now!
25 Years Charter Fishing Experience

The ad is not Jacksonville-specific. I hesitate but I click on it anyway as it mentions deep-sea fishing in Florida where Jacksonville is located.

I land on a page for charters in Tampa – a 5 or 6-hour drive from Jacksonville, depending on traffic. Am I going to drive there? It's very unlikely, especially since the waters off Jacksonville are known for very good deep-sea fishing.

To add insult to injury, the advertiser *paid* for this ad because I clicked on it, hoping the offer would be Jacksonville-related.

This ad should not be displayed to people searching for deep-sea fishing in Jacksonville.

So it's a lose-lose situation. I got disappointed and the advertiser lost money.

This company did a good job attracting me but failed to convert me to a customer with the ad that was not relevant to my search.

Here is another example of doing a good job on attracting but poor job on converting to customers.

I type "red shoes' in the search box of Google.

The following ad gets displayed

Red Shoes at Sears
www.sears.com/shoes
Save Big on Shoes and Get them
At Sears.com Today!

I click on this ad from Sears and....

…. I land on the page displaying women's cowboy boots -- none of which are red. ☺

It's another waste of money for the advertiser.

One of the challenging aspects of paid search advertising is tracking conversions such as calls made or forms filled out. A lot of efforts go to getting high ranks for paid and organic searches and making sure that conversions happen. Much less attention is spend on making sure that we can track all these subsequent leads – either phone calls or filled out forms. Without proper tracking of leads it is impossible to assess how many sales resulted from these leads or our digital marketing efforts. This is especially true when sales cycles are very long. Therefore, without proper tracking of leads it maybe impossible to assess effectiveness of such advertising and we're back to shooting from the hip.

Last but not least, it's easy to get pay per click wrong if not enough attention is paid to campaign management.

A typical paid per click of PPC campaign is made of combinations of various keywords, ads and landing pages.
The best combinations are selected based on analysis of conversions.

To select the best combination tweaks and changes are constantly being made to ads and landing pages. Various ads and landing pages are being constantly compared to each other with respect to conversion. This is called A/B testing.

So, in a PPC campaign we have three potential points of failure:

- Wrong keyword
- Wrong ad
- Wrong landing page

As simple as this concept seems it's easy to get it wrong due to the variety of factors influencing the outcome.

In my experience, PPC campaigns creation and management is best to be left to experienced professionals.

"Help. I spent $90 on AdWords. 32 clicks and no conversions. Need to pay rent to my mom next week."

It's worth noting that PPC campaign is a great foundation for SEO optimization. A successful PPC campaign will help us to find:

- High performing keywords
- It'll provide us with best ads or listings
- We'll be able to determine which landing pages work the best

In many cases PPC could be used as help with the SEO process. So, sometimes we recommend running a PPC campaign for 3 months to learn how to shape the subsequent SEO campaigns.

4.14

DISPLAY AND REMARKETING ADS

The next type of paid advertisements is called display ads. Let's discuss them in more depth.

The ad may match the content of an adjacent article. For example, we may have Cadillac Escalade ads placed next to the article on SUVs. This is also called a contextual ad.

Behavioral ads are displayed based on user's behavior such as, for example, the number of previous visits to certain websites.

You purchase the number of times you want your ad displayed. You pay for impression not per click, but the ads are still clickable. This concept is also based on real time auction between various advertisers.

Display ads are used mostly for brand building and awareness.

Display ads come in wide range for different formats such as:

- Text
- Images
- Flash
- Video

The advertiser controls:

- Targeting of those ads to different users
- Frequency
- Sequence
- Geography

Display ads can be displayed:

- At the right place
- At the right time
- To the right audience
- At the right price

This is the ultimate digital marketing dream come true.

Have you ever wondered how you may be getting ads from a company after you visited their website?

Here is the schematic of an operation called *remarketing*:

- Users that visit your site each get a cookie, a tiny program installed in their browsers.
- When they leave and visit other sites, including, for example, Facebook, Gmail, and Yahoo, the cookie triggers your ad to be displayed.
- Your ads are being displayed only to your cookie owners, who are previous visitors to your site.
- You can specify the duration and frequency of remarketed ads. But be aware that if they're overdone, it could be perceived as 'e-stalking.'

One visit to your site is typically not enough to convince visitors to take action. Therefore, remarketing gives you a chance to bring an indecisive prospect back to your site. You control who gets what message where and when.

4.15

PAID ADS – CASE STUDY

Now let me walk you through a classical case study on **pay per click** campaign for a startup company.

This is for a manufacturer of roller shutters in Toronto, Canada.

The firm is trying to create a market for roller shutters, which are very popular in Europe but relatively unknown in Canada.

They've equipped their factory, bought a lot of raw materials, and the only thing between them and success is sales. Since this is a new product in the Canadian market and they have not advertised at all, few potential customers are aware of them.

This is their current situation:

- Roller shutters are not selling quickly enough
- Dealers are not generating enough sales
- Owners are concerned about seasonality. With the upcoming winter sales may slow down.
- If the shutters do not sell, the company has to hold off manufacturing
- A plan is needed *now* to get more calls from prospective customers

They have hired a digital marketing agency and communicated a single objective – make the phone ring with qualified buyers!

The agency did an exhaustive keyword search, very similar to keyword searches done for SEO. They came up with 21 variants of window & roller shutters.

The agency proposed a PPC campaign on Google and Bing…

…with professionally written ads and custom built landing pages.

Next, a 2-phase approach was proposed.

In the first phase, to be run for 3 months, the idea was to deliver immediate leads while learning what combination of keywords and ads are the best and to discover if the cost of advertising is not prohibitive.

After 3 months, the decision is to be made whether to continue as is or switch to SEO.

It is a classical approach for new businesses. Run a 3-month exploratory PPC campaign, learn what works, and then use the input for sustainable SEO.

Google AdWords has a tool to select where ads will be displayed. It's quite precise in defining the audience in terms of geography. The decision was made to show ads in a radius of about 100 miles from Toronto.

The agency ran the forecast based on some historical industry data.

It was assumed that 100 searches per day will result in 5 visits to the company's website, which translates to 150 visits monthly.

It was assumed that 2% of these visits would turn into actual sales. The average sale is about $10,000.

The results came close to expectations. In three months, 10 sales were made as a result of this advertising campaign. PPC campaign provided a lot of great information about the best keywords, best ads and best performing landing pages.

The decision was made to switch to SEO as the less expensive option in the long run.

4.16

THE ULTIMATE GOAL

At the beginning of this part we discussed two Golden Rules of digital marketing. The first one was To Find and To Be Found.

The second golden rule was digital marketing ABC, where A stands for Attract, B for Bring and C for Convert. I want to share with you how the second golden rule translates to the ultimate goal of any digital marketing effort.

This concept is based on a very simple table showing the results of digital marketing efforts. The report illustrates the ideal results. The actual numbers presented below are fictional but they represent the most desirable relationships among them. The first column represents the metrics we'll be tracking such as Visits, Engagements, Conversions, Expenses, Revenues and Profits.

The second column represents the Variance between Plan and Actual campaign results.

The two remaining columns depict the plan and actual numbers.

The Ultimate Results of Digital Marketing			
	Variance	Plan	Actual
Visits	3%	1,200,000	1,241,000
Engagements	9%	60,000	65,176
Conversions	19%	3,450	4,112
Expenses	-4%	$300,000	$287,000
Revenue	15%	$567,989	$654,782
Profit	37%	$267,989	$367,782

The first line 'Visits' represents the number of visits to our webpage. Our plan called for 1,200,000 visitors. The actual number was 1,241,000. We have exceeded our plan by 3%. Our expectations were based on the previous campaign but we wrote a better copy for our listing showing in Google search results. More people clicked on our listings. Great! We did a pretty good job attracting visitors to our web pages.

The second line 'Engagements' represents the number of visitors who engaged with our website for, let's say, more than one minute (the definition of what constitutes engagement can be as simple as anybody who did not exit right away). On average, the longer the visitor stays on our website, the better. Our expectations were exceeded by 9% because we posted more relevant content since our last campaign. This means that not only we got more visitors than we expected, but more visitors stayed on our websites longer than we expected (reading more). That's even better!

The third line 'Conversions' shows the number of visitors who 'converted'. Conversion is defined here as making a phone call to a number listed on your website, filling out a form, making a payment, downloading more information or getting an answer via online chat. We exceeded our own plan by 19% because we supplemented the written content with video of our products. This means that not only we attracted more visitors and engagements, but these engaged visitors did something that the digital marketing is all about – they've completed the journey that resulted in sales or leads (by leaving more information on how to reach them). That's the ultimate digital marketing dream!

However, to call this campaign a success, one needs to look at the return on investment (ROI). Here we've achieved the stellar results as well.

'Expenses' were lower than expected. How often does it happen? This may have been a result some tasks done in-house instead of hiring an outside help.

'Revenue' was 15% higher than we've promised due to more visits, more engagements and more conversions.

Therefore, 'Profit' exceeded our expectations by almost 40%!

As I mentioned before, the numbers for 'Plan' and 'Actual' are fictitious but the relationships between them are feasible and desirable. Similar results presented here are the ultimate goal for any campaign (assuming that the 'Plan' numbers were realistic). We did more with less expense and we were able to prove it. How often does it happen?

All these numbers should be available online in real time to be able to react quickly to any undesirable trends. At a minimum we should be able to examine them by products and services we sell, by geography, by customer demographics, such as age, income education. And of course by our own digital marketing channels such as paid ads, search, social media and email; and all of these over any period of time. We need this capability to be able to answer the ageless questions of:

- Who?
- When?
- Where?
- What?

Was purchased as a result of our marketing effort. If we cannot answer these questions it'll be impossible to determine what works and where we should shift our resources. We'll be back to shooting from the hip.

You'd be surprised but today very few companies can do these analysis online and in real time.

I'll be discussing throughout this book why it's hard to come up with such a simple report.

5.0

COMPETITIVE ANALYSIS

The Internet is a great place to find a lot of information. This is especially true for information about competitors.

All of our competitors communicate their marketing messages over the Internet. Thus, all this information is in the public domain and could be explored, summarized, and analyzed with the right tools.

However, this is also a double-edged sword. Our own Internet presence can also be analyzed by *our* competitors.

In this chapter, we'll go over tools and techniques to help us learn as much as possible about our online competitors.

I wanted to share with you my 3 favorite quotes on competitive intelligence. As we can see, the concept of competitive intelligence has been relevant for ages.

The first one is from Sun Tzu – a Chinese military strategist and philosopher who was born about 500 BC. He is known to have said, **"Know your enemy and know yourself; in a hundred battles, you will never be defeated."**

Indeed, ask yourself a question about the value of information when faced with a formidable marketing foe. The more you can learn, the more likely you will be able to formulate the winning strategy.

The second quote is from Mark Twain who succinctly noted, "**It is wiser to find out that suppose.**" We have seen so many marketing campaigns based on suppositions where the actual information was there to grab online.

The third is from a contemporary Dutch business executive who used to be responsible for Royal/Dutch/Shell strategy.

His quote is especially relevant in the context of the Internet. He noted,

"Your ability to learn faster than your competition is your only sustainable competitive advantage."

This is very true, as all the information about everyone's digital marketing activities is out there in the public domain. Whoever can master gathering and analyzing it, will gain a competitive advantage.

There are two core components of competitive analysis:

- Internet Presence Analysis and
- Online Active Listening

The first deals with analysis of competitors' website content, rankings, and social reach.

The second deals with daily listening and analysis of relevant social media posts by all your competitors.

Jointly, the two components allow for a comprehensive understanding of your competitors' Internet marketing positioning.

In the Internet Presence Analysis section, we discuss the overall Online Strategy of selected competitors in terms of:

- Pay per click campaigns and their effectiveness
- Organic Google rankings
- Social media activities
- Mobile presence

Online Active Listening allows us to monitor activities of competitors in real time on:

- Twitter
- LinkedIn and LinkedIn groups
- Facebook
- Google plus
- And key blogs

The problems we're trying to address include:

- Do we know what our competition is doing online?
    o How do they rank in Google?
    o Are they active on Social media?
    o Are they using paid advertising?
    o What is the quality of their website?

This information will tell us a lot about the sophistication of digital marketing of any competitor.

Finding out how many keywords they rank on the first results page in Google will tell us a lot about their strategy. The same holds true if we find out how much they spend on paid ads, and what keywords they use in paid search.

On the flipside, you may discover that your major industry competitors are not active online at all. This is quite typical with traditional B2B businesses that are still learning how to leverage the Internet in their marketing.

- How do we compare?

If we were far behind, we would know that it would take substantial effort to catch up. If we're at par, we may want to think about how to get ahead.

- Where do we start if we have to catch up?

The outcome of a competitive analysis will provide answers to this question at a high level. In reality, there may be a lot of things that we may need to do to catch up. We'll discuss how to prioritize multiple initiatives in our Strategy Chapter.

Typically, we recommend comprehensive comparison of at least 5 competitors on the following:

- Ranking in Google
- Social media activities
- Paid advertising
- Website quality
- Content quality
- Digital marketing strengths and weaknesses

From this picture we'll better understand where we stand compared to our competitors. This will be the basis for recommendations on where to start our digital marketing project.

Completing a competitive analysis provides several benefits:

- We can make more informed decisions.
- As Mark Twain said, "It is wiser to find out that suppose."

- We can achieve buy-in from the whole team.

Successful digital marketing projects are based on very good communication and understanding. Since online marketing terms and concepts could be quite confusing, it's of paramount importance that the team has a common understanding of the scope, objectives, and reasons for certain decisions. Buy-in from the whole team is required to have a chance for success.

- The third benefit is solid input to our budget estimation.

If we have a lot of catching up to do, we need to plan to get more resources. If on other hand, we're already leading the pack online, our current budget may be sufficient.

5.1

INTERNET PRESENCE ANALYSIS

We'll discuss 4 major types of Internet presence analysis examples:

- Manual website audit
- Technical analysis
- Paid ads and organic ranking, including social reach and website and blog content
- Strategic positioning

First, we conduct a Manual Website Audit of the user experience, content message, and ease of navigation.

We use a set of rules for scoring the current state and compare it to the goal.

We look at whether the website content is clear. We evaluate website accessibility and assess how well branding and marketing is handled. We analyze website navigation and content, and verify how many basic elements of Search Engine Optimizations are in place.

Based on the Manual Website Audit, we determine which one of the categories shows the most room for improvement.

Website Success Drivers	Current	Goal
Clarity of Website Content	3.6	5.0
Accessibility	3.5	5.0
Marketing	3.1	5.0
Navigation	3.2	5.0
Content	3.3	5.0
Search Engine Optimization	2.1	5.0

In this example, we can tell that search engine optimization needs improvement as it scored the lowest at 2.1 points.

Next we evaluate technical aspects of the websites. We look at:

- Accessibility Score
- Content Score
- Technology Score
- And Overall Score

	Accessibility Score	Content Score	Technology Score	Overall Score
Your Company	7.7	7.3	5.1	6.7
Competitor A	3.1	6.0	1.7	4.3
Competitor B	7.9	6.0	6.6	7.1
Competitor C	6.5	7.0	5.9	6.8
Competitor D	6.4	6.6	5.8	6.1

Overall, Competitor B shows the highest overall score of 7.1. They are the strongest in two out of three categories, Accessibility and Technology, but Your Company has the highest Content score.

A quick conclusion from this analysis is that 4 out of the 5 companies score pretty close to each other, and the only one lagging behind is Competitor A.

Another finding is that Competitor B needs to be analyzed and watched more closely, as they lead the pack.

The next analysis, Paid Ads and Organic Ranking, compares these 4 statistics:

- Number keywords used in PPC campaigns
- Number of keywords ranked in Google top 20 position
- Number of website pages indexed in Google
- Number of inbound links to the tested website

	# of PPC keywords	# of top 20 position keywords	# of pages	# of links
Your Company	2,036	1,528	2,450	349
Competitor A	-	893	2,710	1,235
Competitor B	-	7,231	9,351	3,158
Competitor C	-	419	1,232	351
Competitor D	-	37,245	52,414	6,630

In this example, we see that only Your Company invests in paid advertising. Your competitors do not. We don't know if it's good or bad until we analyze ROI for the existing paid campaign. If the ROI is positive, your company may lead the pack here.

The quick conclusion from this chart is that Competitor D is doing a very good job on SEO and has a very large site compared to other competitors.

The good job on SEO is denoted by the largest number of keywords they rank on, as well as the largest number of inbound links.

It looks like Your Company has a lot of catching up to do on SEO.

It's interesting to note that Company B showed up on our radar as scoring the highest on technology, but this does not translate to marketing prowess.

Quite frequently, these two aspects are not tied to each other. We see a lot of beautiful and technically great sites that are not marketed well online.

Marketing prowess will always win over technical aspects, assuming that the technology meets the minimum requirements for SEO. In other words, beyond a certain point, technical wizardry does not contribute much to lead generation.

Social Media is the Internet's version of "word of mouth." It's very important for B2C companies and less impactful for B2B businesses. Analysis of social media activities can tell a lot about the digital marketing strategy of any company.

Social Reach analyzes how active the companies are on social media sites.

We examine the following:

- Number of Twitter followers
- Number of tweets
- Number of Facebook "likes"
- Number of Google+ circles
- Number of Pinterest followers
- Number of LinkedIn connections
- Number of YouTube subscribers
- Number of YouTube viewers

	# of Twitter Followers	# of tweets	# of Facebook likes	# of G+ circles	# of Pinterest followers	# of LinkedIn connections	# of YouTube subscribers	# of YouTube viewers
Your Company	1,340	5,879	3,490	44	-	876	1,820	7,909
Competitor A	4,209	8,993	128	65	554	870	8,780	5,609
Competitor B	3,200	7,458	20,190	634	301	45	3,098	12,986
Competitor C	2,459	3,997	3,200	301	-	125	2,093	4,890
Competitor D	13,067	12,987	4,390	1,267	1,278	1,980	4,987	3,987

This table reveals different marketing strategies among the competitors:

- Competitor D is betting on Twitter – they dominate this media.
- Competitor B seems to bet more on Facebook and YouTube where it has the most viewers among all analyzed competitors.
- Competitor D also leads in activities on Google+, Pinterest, and LinkedIn.

In summary, this chart confirms the two previous ones. Competitor D and B are serious players with strong but different social media presence (Twitter versus Facebook and YouTube).

Now let's analyze Website and Blog content.

Content is extremely important. Google will rank your website pages higher if you have good, informative content.

Here we analyze the actual number of content pieces on the current website:

- The current number of pages,
- The number of pages added in the last 12 months,

- The total number of blog posts and blogs added in the last 12 months,
- The total number of PDFs,
- The total and number of Images.

	Your Company	Competitor A	Competitor B	Competitor C	Competitor D
Site Content	2,450	2,710	9,151	1,232	52,414
Site Content (12 months)	172	411	23	189	3,887
Blog Content	40	3,786	9	973	5,299
Blog Content (12 months)	3	388	-	87	162
PDFs	1	3	14	-	975
Images	2,100	1,930	12,334	13,754	43,456

As expected, Competitor D dominates in the content, blogging, PDFs, and Images categories; however, we see that Competitor A added the largest number of blogs in the last 12 months among all tested competitors. Something to watch for? Have they started a catch-up game?

In the following diagram we show the positioning analysis in a strategic format.

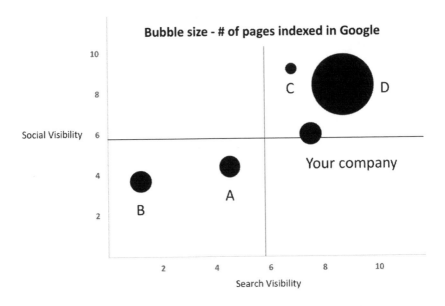

On the x-axis we show Search Visibility or search score, and on the y-axis we show the Social Reach score. The size of the bubble represents the number of pages indexed in Google.

Here again, we can see that Competitor D is an absolute winner and Competitor B has to do a lot of work to catch up with the rest of the companies.

"Your Company" is not doing too badly. It is positioned in the High Search/High Social Reach quadrant. Getting more content may be an important part of a viable strategy to catch up with Competitor D.

It's very important to have your website mobile-ready. Relevant information, such as a phone number to call to reach you or a form to fill out to ask for information on your product or service, should display well on smartphones and tablets and be easily accessible and clickable.

We include a test of mobile readiness in the Internet Presence Analysis. With the growing percentage of searches starting on smartphones, it's imperative to make sites mobile-ready as soon as possible.

5.2

ACTIVE LISTENING

So far, we have examined the analysis of competitors' websites. We demonstrated that we could learn a lot about the strengths and weaknesses as well as the various strategies of our competitors. But this summary analysis was limited to websites and social media activities.

With the growing importance of social media, we need to be able to listen and analyze the ongoing communication of our competition on social media channels.

The challenge is that there is so much communication it's prohibitive to pay attention to every tweet, post, or blog.

Here again, a very powerful and inexpensive software system comes to the rescue. We will discuss an example of a social listening system you can set up yourself at very little cost.

Let's imagine a sales rep from a hypothetical software company selling to large hardware companies such as Dell, HP, IBM, and Lenovo.

The software will produce four columns displaying all the recent tweets relevant to these businesses.

In the first column, we may have all the recent tweets that mentioned word 'Dell'. This includes, for example, tweets to and from Dell, as well as anywhere the word 'Dell' was used. In addition to tweets, this tool can display any mention of Dell on other social media, blogs, recent articles, YouTube videos, and so on.

So a sales rep can quickly review the feed on Dell in preparation for a sales call there.

In addition, we can group various columns into tabs.

These tabs are created to group information by customers, prospects, competition- companies, competition-products, trade shows, industry, and opinion leaders.

They can be configured for sales people, or salespeople can configure them themselves. Some tabs can be private and some designated to be shared with the team.

In this case, our hypothetical company competes with major CRM vendors; salesforce.com sugar and act. For each of them, one stream or column was created. There's a lot of information in these streams that could be quite valuable to a sales rep. It includes promotions, job offers, opinions, stock prices, and etcetera – a lot of sales intelligence that can help to position or close the deal.

We can also focus on what industry opinion leaders are doing with respect to their social media presence. This may be more relevant to marketing than sales; but nevertheless, it gives us access to the top thinkers in the industry.

Since all of them have social media presence themselves – nowadays it's impossible to be an industry expert with no social media -- we can find out a lot about the latest thinking, fads, and trends. This was unthinkable only a few years ago, but now we have almost direct access to the most recent trends in our industry.

In summary, monitoring social media may lead to a variety of discoveries; for example:

- Social media activities by competitors -- what and how it's being used
- A new player entered the market
- A new product is offered by a competitor
- Quality problems -- both your own and those of competitors
- PR issues
- A Key customer, prospect, or competitor is in financial trouble
- An emerging technology trend
- New regulations

Active listening to social media is highly valuable to marketing as an input to strategy, tactics, and execution.

It's equally important to sales people, especially in B2B businesses, where complex and long sales cycles require constant monitoring of external factors that can impact the sale.

Setting up social media listening for sales professionals will help them greatly in:

- Preparing for sales calls
- Reviewing the prospect's and competitors' activities on
  - LinkedIn
  - Twitter
  - Facebook
- Engaging with prospects
- Communicating with existing customers

In summary, setting up competitive intelligence capabilities is of paramount importance. It's very inexpensive to set up such a process now, compared to manual alternatives from just a few years ago.

The benefits include:

- Intelligence on the current digital marketing efforts by major competitors
- Internal education and buy-in

- Sales intelligence
- Input for strategic planning
- Input for budget planning

6.0

READINESS INDEX

We're going to take a health check of our own website. It'll be like going to a doctor for an annual checkup visit. Nobody wants to do it but the consequences for not doing it may be dire. We'll perform this health check using the Internet Readiness Index, a unique method to evaluate technical aspects of any website.

Here it's how it works.
We score any website from 0 to 10 for four major categories:

- Accessibility – how easy it's to access your website
- Content – how relevant is your website content
- Marketing – how good is your marketing message
and Technology – how good is the technology used to build your site.

Overall Summary	4.4
Accessibility Summary	3.5
Content Summary	6.4
Marketing Summary	4.5
Technology Summary	1.5

In this example these four categories made up the overall score of 4.4. Then we'll examine multiple sub-categories to provide detailed feedback on any possible improvements.

I'll discuss these sub-categories in more detail as we go.

Technical aspects of your web presence are extremely important. Let me give you two examples. You can have the best SEO setup in the world but if your website pages load too slowly you'll not show up on the first page of search results. Google and other search engines know if your pages are loading too slowly and they'll penalize you for slow response.

In addition, an average attention span of any Internet user is about 3 seconds. If the requested page loads longer than the user will just abandon it and engage with a fast loading page of your competitor. So a slow website costs you dearly, both in rankings as well as visits and conversions. a page if it takes longer than 3 seconds to load. However, most of website owners don't know of don't track the speed of their own website pages.

The second example is equally telling. You may have broken links on your website without knowing it. What it means that some of the links on your website lead to nowhere and visitors get the infamous 'Page not found – 404 error.' As a result, your users will lose confidence and/or abandon your site. One way or another your conversions will suffer. Here again, most of the website owners have no way of knowing if they have broken links. Broken links happen especially when you keep adding pages to your website.

These are just two most important examples.

There are other technical aspects that impact users experience, such as
- Ease of sharing
- Printing
- Mobile readiness
- Spelling and grammar

All these if not paid attention to may impact SEO and result in lower conversions. Users will be less likely to engage when faced with poor grammar, spelling errors, and reading level that is too hard to understand. Who would buy anything fro a website with spelling and grammar errors?

The Internet Readiness Index measures strengths and weaknesses of many aspects of your website. Think about them as a value-added chain.

As with any chain your chain is only as strong as the weakest links.

You may have invested millions of dollars in the best web presence, but one trivial, mundane technical detail may prevent you from reaching your goals. Traditional marketing has never involved attention to real time technical and operational issues. Now, the best marketing idea can be completely derailed by what may be a small, mundane technical detail.

Therefore, we need to equip website owners with very easy tools to monitor their site quality on the ongoing bases. The analogy here is the automatic detection system in most of our cars today. When something goes wrong with the engine we get a flashing light on our dashboard. We're not expected to be car mechanics to drive our cars. Too much investment is riding on small details to let it go unattended.

Most website owners don't know what they don't know. They have no way of knowing if their website has any technical deficiencies. This is especially true for websites with many pages and a lot of updates. It's also true for websites hosted on third party servers.

The best practice calls for being able to monitor technical aspects of your website on the regular basis—especially page loading times and missing or broken links. The only way to know it is to use the right tools and processes.

Internet Readiness Index can be used in several ways. The first way we already discussed is to test your website implementation and performance, taking a high level health check. Another use is for competitive analysis. We can run this Index on multiple competitive websites and get a lot of analysis done by comparing them to each other.

We can use it to:

- Analyze SEO problems,
- Prioritize enhancements
- Communicate with non-technical executives.

This format that I'm showing here is easy to understand for non-technical people.

And last but not least it could be used as a baseline to measure improvements. It's probably not that important where you score today, I think it's much more important to have a tool that establishes a baseline that will help us to measure our progress as we move along in our digital marketing efforts.

6.1

READINESS INDEX CASE STUDY

Let's now examine health check results in more detail.

Overall Summary	4.4
Accessibility Summary	3.5
Content Summary	6.4
Marketing Summary	4.5
Technology Summary	1.5

Here are the top results for a multi-billion dollar transportation company specializing in moving goods around the United States using large trucks.

As you can see here, this company's website is not enjoying perfect health.

The Overall Summary of the website score is Poor: 4.4 out of 10.

The sub-scores are also quite poor, with the exception of the content score where this company earned 6.4 out of 10 points.

Let's discuss in more detail all four sub-scores that make up the Overall score.

Internet Readiness Index - Accessibility Summary: 3.5

First, it is Accessibility summary. It measures how accessible the website is to people with disabilities, users on mobile phones, and other devices.

Warning signs	Positive feedback
Uses tables for layout	Alt text is used
Not W3C compliant	URLs are clear
Headings are not defined	
One link broken	

Each of the test results comes with key points and they are broken down into warning signs and positive feedback.

On the warning signs, we can see that this website uses tables for layouts. Without going into more technical detail, this tells us that the website has been built with very outdated technology and it's ready for a major overhaul.

The second test, W3C compliant it's also about lack of adherence to certain technical standards. This means that the site may not be compatible with most browsers.

The third one about the Headings not defined it's more serious one as it has an impact on both SEO and how well your website can be navigated by people with disabilities. If you don't have headings they can't be read automatically to people who are visually impaired.

This fourth section alerts us to a broken link. When a user clicks on a broken link, a 'Page Not Found' error message is displayed. Broken links have very negative impact on user experience as well as SEO

On the positive side, it looks like alternative text is being widely used.

That's a technique to help blind users navigate. Basically, there are software packages that read aloud the text description associated with posted pictures. Also, alternative text, if well written, helps with SEO. As a general rule, picture descriptions should contain at least one of the keywords on a given webpage.

The URLs are fairly clear and self-explanatory instead of using a lot of special characters and cryptic technical terms with no meaning to an average user.

Internet Readiness Index - Content Summary: 6.4

Warning signs	Positive feedback
Updated occasionally	Heavily shared socially
	Content matches keywords quite well
	Includes contact details

Content Summary score is Good. This test measures the quality and volume of content on this website. We see that the content could be updated more often than it is.

On the plus side:

- Content is shared through social media,
- It matches keywords well,
- It includes detailed company information.

Warning signs	Positive feedback
Ranks poorly in search engines	Heavily shared socially
Not on Facebook	Content matches keywords quite well
Not on Twitter	Quick to load
Decreasing in popularity	Reasonably well linked to
No Analytics is used	URLs are fairly clear

The Marketing Summary score, however, is poor. Marketing score tells us how well this website is marketed online. This includes SEO and social marketing.

We already know from this test that this company doesn't rank well in search engines.

It's not on Facebook or Twitter either. This doesn't mean that they don't have Facebook or Twitter accounts. It means that there are no links to Facebook or Twitter from their website.

The site is decreasing in popularity.

And a lack of Analytics indicates that the site is not being monitored for the number of visits or conversions. Therefore, this website is probably not being used as a significant source of leads.

There are, however, many links from Facebook and Twitter pages to this site. This would lead me to believe that this company is investing in more online activities on Facebook and Twitter as compared to their own website.

However, a best practice of digital marketing is for the website and social media to work jointly to generate leads.

- The content matches keywords well.
- The site loads quickly.
- There is a reasonable number of links to the site.
- And the URLs are clear.

Internet Readiness Index - Technology Summary: 1.5

Warning signs	Positive feedback
Errors found	Quick to load
Uses tables for layouts	Alt text is used almost everywhere
No Analytics is used	URLs are fairly clear
Headings are not defined	
Not W3C compliant	

The Technology Summary score is Very Poor. It's the lowest score of all, at 1.5.

There are a lot of technical problems with this site. The site is outdated and not well maintained.

The major problems on this site include:

- Errors, indicating technical problems,

- Tables used for layouts instead of style-sheets

- Lack of Analytics,

- Headings are not defined

- And the site is not W3C compliant.

Internet Readiness Index - Recommendations

Importance	Description	Test
5	Consider adding fresh, relevant content more often.	Freshness
4	Consider using a website analytics solution, such as Google Analytics (which is free).	Analytics
4	This website should be made responsive, i.e., suitable for mobile and tablet devices.	Mobile
4	Consider a complete rebuild of the site. This website appears to have been built using very out of date technologies (tables), suggesting a rebuild is overdue.	Stylesheets

The Internet Readiness Index software provides automatic recommendations. This slide shows an example of recommendations for improving website design. Some helpful tips are:

- Add fresh and relevant content often

- Enable Google Analytics

- Make the website responsive so it can be viewed on smartphones and tablets

- Rebuild the website using the newest technologies.

7.0

ANALYTICS INTRODUCTION

Let's talk about analytics now or how to measure results of our digital marketing efforts.

This important chapter is devoted to the goals and techniques we use to measure the results of our digital marketing efforts.

It's the heart and soul of any digital marketing campaign. Without these tools, we're shooting from the hip and not taking advantage of the single largest benefit of digital marketing.

On the other hand, we can use these tools and techniques to calculate the indisputable return on investment for our digital efforts. This leads to better resource allocation and more profitable operations.

As we mentioned in the Foundations chapter, we're in the midst of the measurement revolution. The rapid decrease in the price of software, hardware, and telecommunications allows us to collect, store, and aggregate massive amounts of data; however, all this data is useless unless it's analyzed.

For the first time in the history of marketing we can measure the real ROI of any digital campaign.

In other words, we can attribute incremental sales to a specific ad or campaign.

But this is only possible if we have the right system in place. I'll be talking about it in more depth later in this chapter.

This is of profound importance to advertisers and consumers. For advertisers, it leads to a lower cost of advertising based on more precise targeting and lower costs compared to print, TV, and radio.

For consumers, it translates to more meaningful and less annoying offers that more closely match their interests -- as well as lower costs for products and services, as savings on advertising are being passed on to consumers. Both sides of the commerce equation are the winners.

The losers of our measurement revolution are traditional advertising channels such as TV, radio and print, whereby it's impossible to measure the impact of a single ad on sales.

Any analysis needs to answer these 5 questions:

- Who?
- What?
- When?
- Where?

And finally

- WHY?

It's much like old-fashioned journalism – the principle is the same.

We collect a lot of granular data and, as a result, we know:

- How many times your ad was displayed
- How many visitors clicked on it and visited your site

- How many visitors bounced immediately versus stayed longer or visited other pages
- How many filled out forms, or made a phone call

… And much more…

We also know:

- Who clicked
- Where they were when they clicked
- What device they clicked on
- What part of the screen they clicked
- When they clicked
- What pages they visited
- What forms they filled out
- What phone numbers they called
- What products they purchased

With the right tools we may be able to answer who, what, when, and where; but it will be up to the knowledgeable analyst who's familiar with your business to answer the question, WHY?

7.1

VALUE ADDED CHAIN

Let me walk you through the business Analysis Value Added Chain

It's made up of 4 components:

- Data
- Information
- Knowledge
- Action

In a general sense, data are the raw numbers in a spreadsheet or database.

Information is born when the raw data is summarized and graphed.

Information becomes knowledge when it's interpreted in the context of other information that may not be available online or print -- but it's instrumental in drawing conclusions.

And finally, all the knowledge in the world is useless unless it's translated to action based on that knowledge.

Let me illustrate that concept based on a visit to a doctor.

Let's say a parent brings in a toddler who is coughing and running a temperature.

- Data

First, the doctor will start collecting all the data, including ordering various tests that will provide raw data points.

- Information

The data from various tests will be transferred to charts and tables, compared with other data in the system, like historical data. This will become information.

- Knowledge

Our doctor will look at this data and, based on his knowledge and the child's physical exam; he may diagnose a strep infection.

- Action

This would be a worthless experience if the doctor didn't write the prescription and parents did not fill it and give the medicine to the child. This is called *action based on knowledge*.

If we apply this model to Internet Marketing the data will be stored in Google Analytics and other social media analytics databases.

It will become information when we chart it, compare it to other values, determine trends, etcetera.

Without an intimate knowledge of the business at hand, it would be very hard to turn this information into knowledge.

We need to call a 'doctor' -- somebody whose experience and knowledge of the business will lead us to the right conclusions.

It's impossible to store all information relevant to the business analysis in one homogenous database. For example, in cases such as natural disasters, bankruptcy of the supplier, election results, or changes in currency exchange rates, it's hard to imagine automated decisions anytime soon.

The same goes for regional differences in food or styles. It's hard to imagine a lot of demand today for boiled peanuts outside of the American south, or for black colored toys for kids anywhere in the world. These rules are not codified anywhere, yet they are usually known by experienced marketers.

In addition, may businesses offer very complex products and services, and it's impossible to market them effectively without knowing how they work. And how they work is not codified either.

So, despite all the hype about artificial intelligence, I cannot imagine marketing being done by machines as long as humans are around. To move from information to knowledge, you need experienced human intervention.

To make things even more complex, people with knowledge may not have authority to take actions. This is a very common phenomenon, especially in larger organizations where an experienced analyst is not an executive and cannot make financial decisions without the involvement of higher authority.

In such cases, the effectiveness of a marketing campaign will also depend on the degree of communication and cooperation between an analyst and an executive.

Metrics	Data Source	Comments
Social media shares, fans, followers	Twitter, Facebook, LinkedIn	Hard to automate; usually done by hand
Open rate, clicks rate, new email signups	Email system	How to reconcile
Return visits	Google Analytics	
New visitors	Google Analytics	
Inbound links	Google Search Console	
Time on page	Google Analytics	

Number of leads	Google Analytics and/or CRM	Transfer by hand between GA and CRM
Orders, repeat orders	Google Analytics, ERP, ordering system	Cart abandonment analysis needed
Sales	Google Analytics	
Revenues, average order	CRM, ERP	
Customer referrals	CRM	If collected here

This table depicts the complexity of the actual implementation of an integrated online system performing all these analyses in real time.

The first column, Metrics, lists all the data elements we mentioned already. The second column cites the data sources. It looks like, under the best-case scenario, we need to deal with 6 separate systems to get all the right data!

- Social media
- Email
- Google Analytics
- Webmaster Tools
- In-house CRM & ERP systems

And then we have to put it into a single database and provide reporting and analytical tools to turn this data to meaningful information.

The Ultimate Results of Digital Marketing			
	Variance	Plan	Actual
Visits	3%	1,200,000	1,241,000
Engagements	9%	60,000	65,176
Conversions	19%	3,450	4,112
Expenses	-4%	$300,000	$287,000
Revenue	15%	$567,989	$654,782
Profit	37%	$267,989	$367,782

Remember the simple report we've previously discussed several times?

Now we understand why it's so hard to come up with such a simple report online in real time. In addition to relying on multiple data sources, we also have to make sure that the right costs are allocated among the right channels, which by itself is not always simple.

However, the lack of such a report leads to a lot of time for manual compilation of data and report generation, or it results in failing to understand where the profits are coming from. Either way, without such an analysis, we can't take advantage of the single best benefit of digital marketing: transparent return on investment.

7.3

ANALYTICS SUMMARY

In the summary of this very important chapter:

There are tools on the market that can help you answer the questions: Who? What? Where? When? But it's very hard to answer the question WHY? You need experienced data analyst familiar with your business to draw those conclusions.

There is information value added chain going from Data to Information, Knowledge all the way to Action.

How do we get from the massive amounts of data to meaningful conclusions?

We talked about that good communication calls for good visualization. You have to be able to convey your message to non-technical executives who control budgets.

Finally, if you cannot measure you are back to shooting from the hip and not taking advantage of the best of digital marketing.

The Achilles heel of analytics is poor data quality

For example, we may have a list of sales transaction, which is incomplete due to human error

Very often we do not have relevant data that is needed to for conclusive analysis. We just do not collect the information, which may help explain what happened. As an example, when analyzing sales branches performance we do not have access to information on health of branch managers or their family troubles which may be the single best explanation for poor results.

Information may be just incorrect. Wrong sales amounts, wrong product codes, misspelled names, wrong addresses etc. This usually happens when some data is collected manually.

The data may be not timely enough. If the data is one year old, it will tell us very little about this year performance.

And last but not least the data may not be granular enough. If we need to analyze daily sales and our system provides weekly summaries only, such an analysis is just not feasible.

The poor data quality is very frustrating and most senior managers are not even aware of this underlying problem.

8.0

STRATEGY INTRODUCTION

So far we've learned about the digital marketing industry, the four major channels of digital marketing, how to assess our own readiness to undertake a digital marketing project, and how to assess what the competition is doing online.

These are the building blocks for formulating a digital marketing strategy in the context of our own capabilities as well as the realities of the marketplace.

In this section, we'll discuss the best practices of strategy formulation.

The best strategy is not very useful unless it's translated to tangible project plans. We'll introduce best practices for turning strategy into actual deliverables with positive ROI.

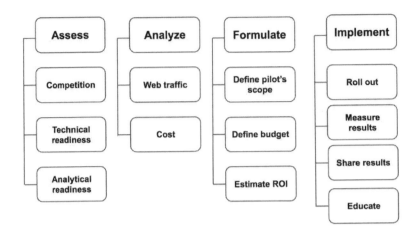

Digital marketing strategy formulation is like any other strategy definition.

First you have to assess your own readiness vis-à-vis your competition. We've introduced these topics in the earlier chapters of our training.

Next you need to analyze existing web traffic to learn where the leads are coming from. We discussed this subject in our Analytics chapter.

Then we need to analyze existing costs and any future investments we can afford. We'll discuss that in more detail later.

I strongly recommend selecting a small project to test the digital marketing waters. Pick up something impactful but relatively simple and limited in scope. Select an initiative that you believe has a high likelihood of success. Estimate ROI and go for funding with a well-documented ROI forecast.

Then it's time for a rollout. Digital marketing projects are like any other complex project. The chances for success are closely related to a good project plan and good project management.

Make sure before you start that you have a clear way to measure results. Your project success will be judged on indisputable numbers.

Digital marketing projects require a lot of cooperation from virtually all business units. Good communication is paramount to the project's success. Make sure you communicate results clearly and educate your audience. The majority of your organization may have little knowledge about digital marketing terms and concepts. Minimize technical jargon and use plain English to communicate.

Strategy formulation is the hardest part of the pilot project. In order to come up with the right strategy, you'll need to combine a lot of technical, business, and financial knowledge in the context of your own realistic capabilities and the realities of the marketplace. It's challenging task, which is why good strategists are highly sought after.

In a nutshell, a good strategy will tell us how to allocate resources among all the channels. At the end of the day, we need to know how much we're going to spend on each channel and what we are going to spend it on.

None of us has unlimited budgets. We need to come up with a rough estimate of what it may cost to deliver.

We've shared with you the average cost of an SEO project in the previous chapter. An average cost of SEO project will range between $30K and $50K for 25 keywords. However, if done in-house, there is little out-of-pocket investment.

Email systems are inexpensive. They seldom exceed a cost of $100 per month in license fees.

Pay Per Click campaigns seldom cost less than $1,000 a month. As a rule of thumb, a PPC campaign for 5 competitive keywords will run about $3,000. These are just rough estimates of the range of investment you can expect to make in PPC. The actual costs will grow with the number of keywords you implement.

Social media involves almost no out-of-pocket investment. It's your time and the time of your team. They're time consuming, but no fees are paid to outside vendors unless you're buying copywriting or copyediting services.

We'll discuss in more detail how to estimate costs later in this chapter.

8.1

STRATEGY FORMULATION

Let's go over each step of strategy formulation in a little more detail.

As far as assessment goes, we need to examine:

- The competition,
- Your own website's technical readiness and mobile presence,
- Your email marketing program,
- Social media presence,
- Existing SEO efforts,
- Existing PPC campaigns.

This will help you define the scope of your pilot program and gain consensus on the project.

You also need to assess your readiness to calculate the actual ROI of your pilot project. I strongly recommend selecting a project where the chances for demonstrating transparent ROI are very high. The pilot project will need to demonstrate positive ROI before it can be called a success.

Make sure you have a process to track leads as well as the ability to estimate actual cost. It's also very important to have a good handle on the lifetime value of a new customer.

This will tell you if you're ready to make transparent, ROI-based decisions

You need to perform a detailed analysis of your current traffic by many variables including, at least, by:

- Keywords
- Hour, day, week, month, and year
- Geography
- Device
- Other segments as discussed in the Analytics chapter.

You need to decide if your pilot project is intended to get more visitors, or to get more conversions, or both at the same time. This is very important, as you have more control over conversions than you have over traffic. Getting more traffic will also be more costly and it will take longer to complete the pilot.

As we discussed before, one of the advantages of digital marketing is that you can start small, measure results, and then expand or abandon based on these results.

Therefore, I recommend starting small and concentrating on low-hanging fruit with a short timeframe and high visibility.

Make sure you gain consensus for your pilot project and manage expectations accordingly.

Position your project as a pilot to learn from and use the results to formulate a broader strategy.

If you can show the pilot's success with a transparent, quantifiable ROI, you will be a hero!

With traditional marketing it was almost impossible to calculate ROI and a lot of guessing was taking place at every step of the project.

Now we have a chance to be guided by objective analytics!

8.2

ASSESSMENT

Let's talk specifics now. This is our unique methodology for strategy formulation.

First, you'll self-assess in 6 key categories of digital marketing strategy based on our scoring guidelines. Next, you'll estimate the recommended investment for several initiatives.

Following that, we'll demonstrate how to prioritize these initiatives. This will serve as the basis for the creation of communication and implementation plans.

	Category	Score	Investment
1	Search engine optimization		
2	Email marketing		
3	Social media		
4	Pay per click		
5	Marketing goals		
6	Analytics		

You'll complete this table based on our scoring guidelines.

Think about your current SEO status and score yourself on a 10-point scale according to the scoring guidelines. These guidelines depict the continuum of the most desired outcomes.

In this example, you get 10 points if your site ranks at positions 1-10 on more than 10 keywords, has nice conversion rates, you're using CRM to track leads, and you can demonstrate positive ROI from your SEO project.

0   Site is not optimized for search engines

1-2 Site ranks on branded keywords only (name of your products, name of your company)

3-4 Site ranks on positions 1-10 for less than 5 keywords but does not provide qualified leads

5-6   Site ranks on positions 1-10 on 10+ keywords but does not provide qualified leads.

7-8 Site ranks as above and enjoys conversion rates to sales and/or qualified leads within an industry standard.

9-10 Leads/sales are being tracked in a CRM system and there is a positive ROI from SEO.

Now think about your current email system and score yourself on this 10-point scale:

Give yourself a score of 0 if no email is being used for leads and sales generation.

1-2 There are some emails for existing customers, but they're not organized in one place.

3-4 There's no repetitive process to collect all prospect and existing customer email addresses.

5-6 There's a repetitive process to collect emails, but no 12-month communication plan or content.

7-8 Communication plan and content are in place, but there's no email marketing software system. Manual rekeying of email addresses between various systems. No analysis on email effectiveness is in place.

9-10 All email addresses along with a 12-month communication plan and relevant content are housed in an integrated email marketing software system. Analysis of email effectiveness is very easy, including open and click-through rates. Email software supports mobile devices. There is positive ROI on email marketing.

Next is your social media positioning. Score yourself with this scale:

Score a 0 if no social media are utilized.

1-2 There are up to 3 social media accounts set up, but they're not being updated.

3-4 Social media accounts are being updated in a haphazard fashion without a clear communication plan.

5-6 Communication plan is in place, but the posting process is manual and there are no social media analytics.

7-8 Communication plan is in place. The Posting process is automated and a review of your own posts can be analyzed. There is capability to actively listen to the competition's social media activities.

9-10 Social media effectiveness measurement is in place (reach, likes, sentiments, etc). It can be demonstrated that social media activities provide a positive ROI.

Use this scale to assess your current Pay Per Click campaign if you run it.

Score 0 if no pay per click campaign is in place.

1-2 PPC campaign is in place, but generates lower than expected traffic.

3-4 PPC campaign generates traffic, but no expected conversions.

5-6 PPC campaign provides sales and qualified leads, but analysis of keywords and campaigns is prohibitive or hard to manage.

7-8 PPC campaign provides expected results and it's easy to manage, including the knowledge of best-performing keywords.

9-10 PPC supplements SEO for total page domination. PPC and SEO have positive ROIs.

Please also note: the lack of pay per click advertising is not necessarily detrimental to Internet Marketing success. But there are situations where it's a very important part of the mix – such as seasonal events, special promotions, branding, and so on.

Use this scale to assess your Internet Marketing goals:

Score 0 if no quantifiable performance goals are in place.

1-2 Some goals are defined, but there's no roadmap to achieve them. Few managers support the need to set goals and track performance.

3-4 Some goals are defined. Some managers have quantified their output, established measurements, and defined ways to achieve them.

5-6 Goals are defined and documented but not communicated throughout the organization. Some managers review progress toward quantifiable goals on a regular basis.

7-8 All managers have established performance goals, documented a roadmap to achieve them, communicated them with subordinates, and review them on a regular basis.

9-10 Goals are established, documented, communicated, regularly reviewed, and tied to the personal compensation of managers and employees.

Setting up goals is not going to cost you anything out of the pocket but it's extremely important part of the overall process. With no quantifiable goals in place it's hard to get good results.

Finally, use this scale to assess your Data Analytics capabilities:

Give yourself a 0 if no data is collected to support an Internet Marketing Plan.

1-2 Some data is available from paper sources.

3-4 Some data is available from paper sources and various electronic files on disjointed and incompatible systems.

5-6 All data is available from various electronic files on disjointed and incompatible systems. Reporting involves exporting to Excel and it's time consuming.

7-8 All data resides in one database but there are no analytical or reporting tools.

9-10 All data resides in one electronic, integrated database allowing for real time ROI calculation.

Remember that this in not only data on traffic, but also sales and profitability. I have never worked with any organization that could boast a score of 10 on this category!

GREG GUTKOWSKI

8.3

SAMPLE RESULTS

	Category	Score	Investment
1	Search engine optimization	2	
2	Email marketing	9	
3	Social media	3	
4	Pay per click	5	
5	Marketing goals	2	
6	Analytics	5	

This table shows typical results for many companies.

1. They rank in Google on branded keywords only – their company or product name.
2. Most companies have good email marketing systems in place.
3. Social media accounts are updated from time to time with no clear communication plan.

4. If they advertise online, they may have a hard time understanding what works, even if the program generates leads, so they lack the knowledge to improve it.
5. As far as marketing goals, this is where a lot of companies are: Some goals are defined, but there's no roadmap to achieve them. Few managers support the need to set goals and track performance. The likelihood of reaching undefined and unstated goals is very low.
6. Most companies struggle with analysis of traffic, sales, and profits.

Now it's time to estimate the recommended investments. This will help us with prioritization, communication, and implementation.

We recommend using another 10-point scale to estimate the level of investment needed to bring each channel to the desired state. 1 will be very easy to do – minimal out of pocket expenses. 10 would be the hardest and the most expensive.

Select a low hanging fruit, get the consensus and subsequently communicate the vision.

	Category	Score	Investment
1	Search engine optimization	2	6
2	Email marketing	9	1
3	Social media	3	3
4	Pay per click	5	1
5	Marketing goals	2	1
6	Analytics	5	9

This table illustrates a typical result of scoring using our methodology.

Let's analyze these results:

The lowest score of 2 was on the Marketing Goals where we agreed that there are no quantifiable goals for your organization with respect to digital marketing.

It will cost no money out-of-pocket to address this deficiency. It may involve a lot of soul searching and bring about the focus, but this is a task with no additional cost. Therefore the cost is estimated to be 1 on the scale from 1 to 10.

SEO also received a very low score of 2. It needs a lot of attention and could be a larger project depending how many keywords will be implemented. Therefore the relative investment is estimated at 6.

The third lowest score is for social media – 3. It is not too hard to address this deficiency just by creating a 12-month communication plan and getting inexpensive software to post blogs to various accounts. Therefore we estimate this effort to be 3.

There are 2 categories estimated at 5.

With respect to PPC, it won't take a lot of effort to understand what works and what does not. But this understanding is crucial to ensure that our budget is spent wisely. PPC is also the easiest to calculate actual ROI, the requirement to get 10 points.

Analytics will be expensive due to the need for data integration. We'll discuss this in more detail in the last chapter of our training.

We're happy with email marketing and there is very little more we can do to improve it.

Here are sample recommendations in order of suggested priority:

1. Don't change much with email marketing – you're doing just fine.
2. Define and communicate digital marketing goals. It costs you nothing, but it sends a clear message about priorities and leads to buy-in.
3. Analyze and possibly improve PPC results. You're already spending some of your budget on PPC, but you're not sure if you're getting your money's worth. It will cost you nothing out of pocket, but PPC could make you a hero.
4. Define a social media communication plan for the next 12 months and get a cheap subscription to Hootsuite or some other social media management software.
5. For SEO, define a small, 5-keyword pilot and measure results. Depending on your skill set, you may need to hire an outside agency for this.
6. Start exploring marketing automation software packages to save time on tasks as well as analytics. Some of them provide almost all the necessary integration out-of-the-box. However, they come with a steep learning curve and tend to be expensive.

The Ultimate Results of Digital Marketing			
	Variance	Plan	Actual
Visits	3%	1,200,000	1,241,000
Engagements	9%	60,000	65,176
Conversions	19%	3,450	4,112
Expenses	-4%	$300,000	$287,000
Revenue	15%	$567,989	$654,782
Profit	37%	$267,989	$367,782

Ultimately, we need to get to the point that this report is easily available online and allows for a quick analysis of profitability of all digital marketing initiatives.

By now we all know that this is not that easy to accomplish. Nevertheless the lack of such capability may prevent us from optimizing all of our digital marketing efforts.

In the next chapter we'll discuss the challenges of system integration and how it impacts your digital marketing efforts.

9.0

SYSTEM INTEGRATION

In this chapter we'll discuss system integration. You may ask what this has to do with digital marketing. Why I should worry about it as a marketer?

Isn't that the domain of Information Systems?

Yes, and no.

Digital marketing involves a lot of software tools that generate a lot of data that does not reside in one place, which makes it hard to analyze.

Whether we like it or not, data analysis is the main driver of all of our efforts and if we can't analyze, we're back to the days of shooting from the hip.

Let me illustrate this challenging problem and opportunity from two perspectives:

- From a sales professional
- From the financial and IT perspective.

Let's start with taking a look at a day in the life of a B2B sales-professional who's trying to hit a sales target.

Let's look at typical daily activities of a sales rep and software associated with those activities.

Activity Type	Software
Make a call	CRM and/or IVR
Take notes	CRM
Send email	CRM and/or email system
Review prospect/customer web activities	Social media sites, Marketing Automation Software, CRM
Engage on Twitter, LinkedIn, Facebook etc - posts, discussions, groups	Marketing Automation Software or direct visits to each social media site
Post a blog	Direct or via Marketing Automation Software
Write a proposal	CRM, document management
Review orders, returns, sales volumes	ERP
Status of open service tickets	ERP and ticketing system
Take order	ERP

When a sales rep makes a call, he will open a CRM to log the call there. The call can also be logged automatically by the phone system – IVR.

When he takes notes he will do it in the CRM system.

When he sends an email, it may be directly from Outlook or Gmail not necessarily integrated with CRM. That would be another system.

When he wants to review a customer or a prospect web activities he'll have to visit social media sites, one at a time or look up at his Marketing Automation software or CRM, unlikely but possible.

When he wants to engage in Twitter, LinkedIn, and Facebook to do posts, participate in discussions or groups he can use Marketing Automation software, but most likely he'll visit each media sites directly.

To post a blog it's most likely he'll go directly to a blog site or use Marketing Automation software.

To write a proposal he'll use a CRM or document management system or ERP. Most likely it'll be a word document stored on his hard drive.

When he wants to review a status of an order, returns, sales volumes he'll use ERP.

If he wants to look up status of an open ticket he'll use ERP or CRM or ticketing system.

Finally, when he wants to take an order he'll log in to an ERP system.

As you can see the sales person will have to log in and log out to at least 6 separate systems during a day.

I know of no single company that offers a single, fully integrated system. Some CRMs are going this way but it's hard to have all the functionality in one system. Marketing automation systems concentrate on campaign management not on an individual prospect. The CRM vendors are trying to pick up a little more marketing automation functionality and Marketing Automation system are trying to pick up a little CRM functionality.

Today's reality is that there are multiple sign-ins. Even with a single password a sales rep has to use various systems. Often a sales professional integrates information by hand, looking up different systems one at a time.

Time spent on manual data integration is time not spent on selling.

Ask yourself – what percentage of sales professional time is spent on manual data integration instead of selling? Sometimes this number exceeds 50 percent. This means that we're paying a lot of money for clerical tasks done by sales professionals.

Now let's take a look from an IT perspective.

Information Type	Technical Source
Basic demographics	CRM (salesforce.com, ACT, Sugar, etc.)
Notes on prospects and customers, proposals	CRM, document management
Inbound/outbound calls stats	Interactive Voice Response IVR/PBX or CRM by hand tracking
Emails sent	CRM and/or email systems
Twitter, LinkedIn, Facebook, etc. - posts, discussions, engagements	Various social media APIs
Website customer visits (what pages, info was reviewed and when)	Google Analytics (or other web traffic analysis tools)
Website activities (downloads, sign ups, chats, purchases)	Google Analytics
Orders, returns, sales volumes, status of customer service tickets	ERP and/or ticket tracking software

In order to perform conclusive sales analysis, we need to integrate a lot of systems. Let's examine the types of information we need and the technical source for each of them.

Basic customer demographics is stored in CRM systems such as saleforce.com, ACT, Sugar, etc.

Notes on prospects and customers, copies of proposals can be stored in CRM or document management systems.

Statistics on inbound and outbound calls can be stored in IVR, PBX, and CRM systems or can be tracked manually.

Emails sent can be tracked by CRM and email systems.

As far as social media activities, Twitter, LinkedIn, Facebook posts, discussions, engagements we'll have to tap to outside databases from social media sites through their APIs.

Website customer visits data will come from Google Analytics or other web traffic analysis tools (sometimes homegrown systems).

Other website activities such as downloads, signups, chats, purchases will be stored in Google Analytics.

Orders, returns, sales volumes, and status of customer service tickets will be stored in ERP and ticket tracking systems.

The only solution to integrate all sales data is to put the relevant information into a single data warehouse. A lot of companies have them but often the data is:

- Incomplete – lack of web activities for example
- Inaccurate – no all systems provide pristine data
- Not synced n time – dome data updated daily vs. weekly or monthly

So far, we've talked only about web traffic and sales analysis.

Profitability analysis will require bringing in financial data, with all the challenges associated with it.

To provide campaign and/or customer profitability by product, geography, demographics, and time, we need to integrate data from at least Web analytics, ERP, and Accounting systems.

Return on Investment analysis brings about challenges associated with cost allocation. Are we looking at direct cost? Is the cost data fully loaded in to database? What's a definition of gross margin versus net margin? How do we define and allocate interdepartmental charges?

A consistent ROI definition should be established and used for comparisons across the campaigns and over time. Otherwise it's like comparing apples and oranges.

There is a need for strong IT and marketing department partnership. It's of paramount importance that these two departments work well with each other. They depend on each other more and more.

Rapid technology changes impact the new ways to market, for example mobile advertisement on smartphones.

Traditional marketers are not technologists and they are not good/don't like data analysis.

Traditional IT shops have a shortage of data analysis skills.

The conclusion – companies need to beef up business analysis skills to bridge IT-Marketing gap.

System integration is costly, but the lack of it is even more expensive.

We need to integrate all of these systems to be able to have our Ultimate Goal of Digital Marketing report available online, real time for analysis of our marketing efforts. Without this simple, but extremely powerful report we won't be able to take advantage of the latest and greatest digital marketing technologies.

The Ultimate Results of Digital Marketing			
	Variance	Plan	Actual
Visits	3%	1,200,000	1,241,000
Engagements	9%	60,000	65,176
Conversions	19%	3,450	4,112
Expenses	-4%	$300,000	$287,000
Revenue	15%	$567,989	$654,782
Profit	37%	$267,989	$367,782

10.0

DIGITAL MARKETING SUMMARY

Let's summarize what we've learned.

We introduced the Digital Marketing Framework, a depiction of various digital marketing channels working in concert with traditional methods.

We went over SEO concepts, paid ads, email, and social media, as well as the technical aspects of your website.

We've discussed how to turbo-charge your traditional marketing with the latest and greatest tools and concepts.

We introduced the two golden rules of digital marketing.

1. The first rule is how to find and be found in the digital haystack that is the Internet.
2. The second rule deals with digital marketing ABC -- how to Attract, Bring, and Convert your Internet traffic.

We discussed that we're in the midst of the measurement revolution brought about by the ongoing decreases in the price of technology, which led to the ability to move, store, and analyze massive amounts of data on line in real time.

We talked about the need to equip expensive professionals with less-costly software tools.

We discussed the challenge of absorbing never-ending changes when we all have limited capacity to process all the changes.

The only way to manage this constant change is to follow repeatable processes and the best practices of digital marketing.

	Category	Score	Investment
1	Search engine optimization	2	6
2	Email marketing	9	1
3	Social media	3	3
4	Pay per click	5	1
5	Marketing goals	2	1
6	Analytics	5	9

We provided you with an actionable framework to formulate your strategy and estimate your budgets.

This framework will help you in strategy formulation, getting consensus, and communicating results.

The Ultimate Results of Digital Marketing			
	Variance	Plan	Actual
Visits	3%	1,200,000	1,241,000
Engagements	9%	60,000	65,176
Conversions	19%	3,450	4,112
Expenses	-4%	$300,000	$287,000
Revenue	15%	$567,989	$654,782
Profit	37%	$267,989	$367,782

Last but not least, we talked about the need for simple online analysis of our digital marketing efforts. We discussed in detail why it's so hard to come up with such a simple report. A big part of the problem in producing this report is the lack of integration among various digital marketing tools.

We stressed several times that one of the best aspects of digital marketing is transparent tracking of results. If we can't measure, we can't manage our digital campaigns in the optimal way.

PART III

SALES

1

INTRODUCTION

In sales, information is power. This is especially true the larger the sale and the more decision makers and influencers are involved.

Sales intelligence can be greatly enhanced by monitoring the social media activities of prospects and competitors as well as real time tracking of web visitors. Sales and ordering processes can be streamlined by using specialty software.

Imagine a 12 month cycle to sell a multimillion dollar contract to a Fortune 1000 company. On your end, beside yourself as a sales executive, there could be several more people in your organization who are involved: a product specialist from corporate, local pre-sales consultant, your manager, and your office administrative support staff.

On the other side of the transaction, there is a selection committee made up of 10 members who meet once per month. The members range from a VP to their admin person. In the process, you have to answer 40 questions on the RFP (request for proposal). You will be communicating via email and phone with most of the members.

How are you going to manage this process, track all this information over 12 months, and continually report progress to your anxious manager waiting for your big possible win to hit the books so the whole branch can get the annual bonus?

We will discuss the two key social media platforms that are the most beneficial in selling: LinkedIn and Twitter. In addition, we will explore several software tools in the digital sales toolbox:

- Google Alerts for staying actively informed by leveraging the Google search engine .
- Hootsuite to do active listening of social media posts by prospects, competitors, partners, and customers.
- Feedly to find good current articles to share with prospects and clients.
- Evernote to keep all the notes on all possible sales-related subjects together.
- Email—a very important sales tool that can be used for communication, education, archiving, and as a to-do list, among other things. The effective use of email can make or break a deal .
- Last but not least, we will discuss CRM or Customer Relationship Management systems such as salesforce.com to manage long sales cycles and ongoing customer service.

There is a growing trend to combine a lot of functions mentioned above in one integrated system. The new term for this is Marketing Automation. We will go over the pros and cons of the integration of so many systems into one.

2

LINKEDIN AND TWITTER

Do you remember the times before social media? All we had was TV, radio, and print media—newspapers and magazines.

The flow of information was mostly one way. From the editors to the public. There were some letters to the editors, but only a few of them got printed.

A group of journalists led by the editorial staff decided what got published, discussed, and promoted. The media were all financed by advertising placed in their publications. Some also charged subscription fees.

They had tremendous power to shape the public discourse, opinion, tastes, and trends. They still do, but that power is eroding at the hand of social media.

Around the year 2000, Internet technologies became so inexpensive and user friendly that anyone could create and publish their own content to the world. You could get a free account on a blogging site and start writing your blog that could be visible globally. The only investment needed was your time. There was no advertising involved.

In 1999, according to Jesse James Garrett, there were 23 blogs on the Internet. By the middle of 2006, there were 50 million blogs according to Technorati's State of the Blogosphere report.

Blogs provided space for comments and the author of a blog could respond to them right there online. This is how the real time interaction between the authors and the audience started. Blogging exploded worldwide.

Then another idea was born. How about if we allow authors and readers to easily connect and stay connected with each other outside of blogs?

Blogging interfaces did not make it easy to stay in touch with all like-minded readers. All you could do was leave your comment and your name on somebody else's blog.

Thus, the new idea was to allow everyone to create their own profile where they could specify basic demographics such as location, age, gender, interests, and hobbies and then let people connect with each other permanently based on those demographics and interests.

Therefore, if I live in Chicago and I am interested in the Chicago Bulls, I could connect with everyone in that city who loves basketball and start reminiscing online about Michael Jordan. I can start an online Chicago Bulls fan group. I may also have other interests and join a group of folks exchanging the best Italian food recipes. This is how social media was born.

This was a completely new channel that did not exist before. It was as revolutionary as the Gutenberg press.

Before the Gutenberg invention, only the rich and influential could own books, as they were very expensive to produce manually. Gutenberg's invention made the book production process much less expensive and thus books proliferated widely.

History likes to repeat itself – the same mechanism worked again when the decreasing cost of media production led to the proliferation of that media.

'Social' in English means communal, collective, popular, civil, public, societal. It also means party, gathering, and get-together. So the social media started as a global collective party facilitated by free and easy-to-use social media platforms. It expanded beyond private discussions to include business discourse as well.

Indeed, participating in social media is very similar to going to a party or a networking event. You can have multiple conversations with multiple people on multiple subjects. You will be popular if you yourself are interesting and a good listener. You will not have much success if you talk about yourself all the time.

Think about social media as a digital word-of-mouth turbocharged by the Internet. The entire positive buzz will be super-sized, but any negative opinions will reach a much larger audience as well.

In this section we are going to discuss Twitter and LinkedIn. They have common, basic functionalities and are made up of two major building blocks. The first block is your profile where you list your name and other demographics, and your interests. The second building block is a way to publish your posts. The common functionality is the ability to connect your profiles with each other and to see your respective posts automatically, including interacting with each other by commenting, liking, sharing, etc.

There is another common thread among all these social media platforms. On all of them, we share tons of information on ourselves, our businesses, accomplishments, hobbies, education, friends, jobs, and responsibilities.

Never before has so much detailed personal information been accessible on such a large scale. Social media platforms use this information to finance their business model. Since social media sites are free to users, they sell this information to advertisers who gain precision in targeting their ads. Never before could you have effectively found and cheaply advertise to males who live around Chicago, are 55+ years old, and love Michael Jordan and Italian food.

The good news for sellers is that never before has so much detailed information been available for market research, competitive intelligence and due diligence.

The whole idea behind this section is to learn how to harness this gold mine of social media information to better understand our prospective customers, existing clients, and competition. In selling and marketing, information is power. But information only has power when used and applied effectively.

Like a goldmine requires sifting through tons of rocks before you get to a nugget, the social media require sifting through tons of trivia and details before you get to an information nugget you can use in sales.

Let's start learning how we can LinkedIn and Twitter to sell more.

3

LINKEDIN OVERVIEW

Now let's talk about LinkedIn.

- Create your own profile
- Connect with like-minded individuals
- Interact

Technically it works like any other social media platform: you create your profile, connect with like-minded individuals, publish your own posts, and interact with other people by commenting, liking, and sharing their content.

The difference is that we are not watching the Kardashians brag about plastic surgeries in LinkedIn, but we are engaged with fellow professionals on serious topics.

- Live resume
- Few degrees of separation
- Professional discussion groups

The strength and popularity of LinkedIn is related to three major functionalities – live online resume, few degrees of separation, and professional discussion groups.

- Your profile is your live résumé or CV
- Much more powerful than PDF copy
- Multimedia content

- Searchable

First, it's the concept of a live resume. Your LinkedIn profile is really your online professional CV.

And your LinkedIn resume could be much more powerful when compared to a paper or PDF copy of a regular one. It allows you to showcase your multimedia creations, your publications, recommendations given and taken, and endorsements of your skills by fellow professionals. It shows what professional groups you belong to, who you follow, and who follows you.

The richness of your profile provides another benefit. You can easily find professionals by their job titles, the industry and company they work for, tenures, geographies, schools attended, and mutual discussion groups, to name a few.

This also means that you can be easily found by anyone who may be interested in your professional experience such as potential employers, headhunters, and business partners.

- Applying for a job with LinkedIn profile
- Who knows who in your network
- A network effect
- Business news

More and more businesses allow candidates to apply for a job with an electronic LinkedIn resume. It makes the whole process easier and more effective on both sides. I expect that with the recent acquisition of LinkedIn by Microsoft, this practice will be even more popular. Microsoft is present in many businesses already and it would make sense for them to leverage these relationships by making it easier for HR departments to process a multitude of resumes and to make this process more efficient and effective.

The second reason for LinkedIn's power and popularity is related to the ease with which you can find out who knows who in your network. Let's say you want to contact Individual A, who you have never met. When you look up his or her profile, LinkedIn automatically shows you your common connections. So you may find out that the person you want to meet works for your college friend. How hard would it be to make that introduction?

If you have a network of 500 plus professionals, you may be surprised how many times there are only 2 degrees of separations between most professionals in the United States. It is beneficial to both you and LinkedIn to connect online with as many professionals as you reasonably can.

Last but not least, LinkedIn provides business news as well as the ability for any member to write on their publishing platform called 'Pulse'. LinkedIn, like any social media platform, is interested in your spending as much time on their site as possible. To accomplish that, they need to provide good reasons for you to do so.

- Targeting ads based on job titles, responsibilities, tenures, industries, geography, etc.
- Ideal for recruiting and job hunting
- Personal and company profiles

Another reason to use LinkedIn is the precision advertising. Now you can target your ads with unmatched precision based on job titles, responsibilities, tenures, industries, geo-location, etc. Thus, for example, you can take out an ad for IT Directors who work in the insurance industry, reside in Atlanta, and have more than 15 years of experience. That was impossible to determine before LinkedIn.

You may ask yourself why we could not do this on Facebook. There are two reasons: technical and marketing.

The technical reason is that the Facebook profile does not support a professional resume format and therefore does not store the relevant information that you can search on. The marketing reason is that Facebook was designed and marketed as a service to 'connect with friends and family' and not as a professional network. It would be hard for Facebook to reposition itself as a professional network, especially now that LinkedIn has already grabbed a very large percentage of professionals who want to connect online.

You can imagine that LinkedIn is heaven for headhunters and job seekers. Actually, most LinkedIn revenues come from job postings by employers and employment agencies. In the context of this training, we are concentrating on the value of LinkedIn as a sales intelligence and market research tool, but let's not forget that it is being financed by employers seeking the most qualified professionals.

4

LINKEDIN – KEY FEATURES

LinkedIn launched in 2003 and in June of 2016, Microsoft announced it will acquire LinkedIn for about $26 billion. Not a bad payday for the visionary founders.

The founders of LinkedIn envisioned what is obvious now - that there is tremendous value in connecting like-minded professionals worldwide around professional topics.

As of 2015, most of the site's revenue has come from selling access to information about its users to recruiters and sales professionals. LinkedIn is just a goldmine for job seekers, headhunters, and sales people. It's available in 24 languages.

Like other social media platforms, it has two major views - your own profile and the newsfeed.

User Profile

Let's start with an overview of the profile. Think about it like your live electronic resume.

Any profile, or live resume, starts with the summary info including a picture, name, job title, location, industry, current employment, and the most recent education.

On LinkedIn, people in your network are called connections. Your network is made up of your 1st-degree, 2nd-degree, 3rd-degree connections, and fellow members of your LinkedIn groups.

- **1st-degree** - People you're directly connected to because you've accepted their invitation to connect, or they've accepted your invitation. You'll see a **1st** degree icon next to their name in search results and on their profile. You can contact them by sending a message on LinkedIn.
- **2nd-degree** - People who are connected to your 1st-degree connections. You'll see a **2nd** degree icon next to their name in search results and on their profile. You can send them an invitation by clicking **Connect** or contact them through an InMail.
- **3rd-degree** - People who are connected to your 2nd-degree connections. You'll see a **3rd** degree icon next to their name in search results and on their profile.
- **Fellow members of your LinkedIn Groups** - These people are considered part of your network because you're members of the same group. You'll see a **Group** icon next to their name in search results and on their profile. You can contact them by sending a message on LinkedIn or through the group.

'How You're Connected' is one of the most powerful features of LinkedIn. By mousing over that icon, you can discover all connections of all your connections. The more contacts you have, the more likely somebody is connected to your connections. For that reason alone, it's worth building as large of a network as possible.

Each contact shows a summary of all posts published by a particular person or organization. LinkedIn allows users to publish content, which is then visible to all their connections. Examining the frequency and quality of posts can give us greater insight into the interests, sophistication, knowledge, and experience of our contacts.

In addition, you can see names of companies your contact worked for, how long he worked there, and what kind of responsibilities he held.

This is followed by the list of top skills as endorsed by their connections. I'll be discussing how to get and provide such endorsements later. But for now, we can see that a particular individual was endorsed as knowing something about running a startup, for example, by over 99 people. If you recognize anyone who endorsed this individual, just mouse over the picture to learn more about that person. This is very powerful, especially if people who issued the endorsements are well known in the industry.

Following is a summary of your contact's education, interests, organizations, honors, and awards.

Last but not least, we can see all the news organizations and companies that your contact follows. This means that the most current posts from these organizations will show up in your contact's news feed automatically.

- Wealth of information
- Present and past employment
- Schools
- Common connections
- Interest, awards, articles, hobbies
- Relationship building
- All this information is searchable

As we can see, the profile provides a wealth of information about all of your contacts. We have learned so much in very little time. We know where your contact works and used to work, where he went to school, who we share in common as a connection, and his interests, awards, articles, and hobbies. This information is very valuable for building relationships based on common professional and personal backgrounds.

In addition, all of the information is indexed and searchable. I'll discuss it in more detail later, but for now this means that we can find a lot of people like your contact, for example, lawyers living in the Bay Area working in Computer Software industry who graduated from the United States Naval Academy.

News Feed

When you log in to your LinkedIn account - by default you will see your news feed. This is a very similar concept to all social media platforms.

At the very top, I get a confirmation that I am in my account and short info on who viewed my profile recently. This is quite valuable, as it could be an indication of possible interest in my services, company, or most recent posts. By clicking on the number, I can examine who viewed my profile and initiate a conversation, if relevant. This is a great way to build your network. If I am in sales, this may mean that a prospect is doing due diligence on my offer. If I am looking for a job, this may be an indication that a prospective employer is taking time to check me out. What we do with this information depends on circumstances, but you may reach out to someone who is checking you out and politely inquire on how you can be of help.

The news feed is very similar to Facebook and Twitter feeds. Each post allows for sharing, commenting, liking, and following the author.

By hovering over the upper right corner of every update, we can invoke a little down arrow icon allowing us to manage updates - hiding, unfollowing, reporting it, etc.

In summary, the LinkedIn newsfeed is very much like other social media platforms. If you have a lot of connections who are active, you may have a lot of content to go through. Some of this content is ads.

On the other hand, you can discover a lot of valuable information, especially on the most important prospects and business partners. We recommend that you manage your LinkedIn feed in such a way that you can concentrate on the most important connections. Just unfollow folks who are of marginal value or post trivial content. Concentrate on the most important 20% of your contacts.

Groups

A unique feature of LinkedIn is the ability to create and belong to groups of interests. For example, you can create your own discussion group on best practices in customer service. Other members—not just your contacts—can become members of your group.

You can also become member of groups created by other users. You can belong to up to 50 groups. Groups can be opened or by invitation only. Sometimes it may take several weeks before you will be accepted to a group as they are moderated by LinkedIn users—not LinkedIn staff.

Groups are a great place to learn more about your contacts or become a thought leader in your field by posting content and moderating discussions.

Search

'Search for people, jobs, companies, and more' is one of the most powerful features of LinkedIn.

If I want to look for IBM, I will type and then select the entity of my interest. As you can see, we can look for jobs at IBM or people who work there or used to work for IBM in the past.

This is another top reason to join LinkedIn. The search capabilities will save you a lot of time when exploring jobs, business opportunities, or sales prospects.

It allows you to create a list of LinkedIn members who meet certain, even multiple criteria.

Let's walk through a simple search. I will search for anyone who currently works at IBM *and* went to the University of Minnesota *and* works with Big Data. I will type:

- "Big data" in the 'Title' box
- "IBM" in the 'Company' box
- Select 'Current' in the dialog box just below Company
- and type "University of Minnesota" in the 'School' box

I have found 10 professionals who work for IBM, went to my school, and are responsible for big data in one way or another.

The first person I found has 6 shared connections with me. I will click on this link and discover that I personally know two people on this list.

One of them is my old friend. I can call him and ask about his career at IBM.

I've just discovered something I could have not known before. If I am looking for a job with IBM in big data, this discovery is of great value. The same is true if I want to sell something to them. Not only do I know who works there and is directly responsible, but I also know who can introduce me!

I can explore all IBM personnel profiles and try to look for even more reasons to start a meaningful conversation. I can also check their activities on Twitter to learn more about their more personal and recent events.

We can also filter information by relationship - 1st, 2nd or more connections, group membership, years of experience, function, seniority level, interests, and company size. This is a gold mine when prospecting or looking for a job.

For example, I can do a very simple but powerful search for all my 1st level Connections who live within 50 miles of my home. This may be a great list to invite to my upcoming 2-hour seminar. It's unlikely that anyone would drive more than 50 miles to a 2-hour event. It looks like I found over 400 first level connections meeting these criteria in my LinkedIn database!

You can save the searches so you don't have to 'reinvent the wheel' every time. Depending on your LinkedIn membership level, you may have more options to search and save.

I would suggest that you play with this function to get familiar with how it works. It's a top reason to join LinkedIn!

6

LINKEDIN BEST PRACTICES

One of the best practices, which is also the most challenging, is to become a thought leader on LinkedIn. You can do it in three ways.

First you may distribute valuable content relevant to your prospective customer. For example, you may send them a link to an article on a recent favorable mention of their company in a certain magazine. Even if they know about this article, they will appreciate that you know their business and you are paying attention.

You can find relevant content by using content curation sites such as Feedly or Scoop.it. (We'll cover Feedly in more detail later).

The second, harder way is to create your own original content. Not everyone has the time or inclination to write, so this is not for everyone. However, if you can write, this is the best way to establish credibility. If you regularly post your own content on LinkedIn, and that content is perceived to be of value to your prospective and existing customers, you have just established yourself as an expert in the field.

The third and the easiest way is to comment on someone else's posts. Comments that are relevant, honest, and sincere can start meaningful business relationships.

We recommend, too, that you join LinkedIn groups. There are two benefits to joining groups.

The first is that groups join like-minded individuals who engage in discussions that are specific to the group. So a group devoted to Social Selling will most likely discuss social selling topics.

The second is that you can email directly to any group member, even if they are not connected to you. LinkedIn otherwise either restricts or charges for these emails, and this is a way to save on fees paid to LinkedIn. In addition, an email from a group member is more likely to be opened as opposed to a completely cold approach.

- Thought leader
    - Subscribe and curate valuable content
        - Feedly, Scoop.it
    - Create original content
    - Comment
- Join Groups
    - Industry
    - Local
    - Customers
    - Save on InMail

One of the most powerful features of LinkedIn is the ability to search all the users by their business attributes. There is no better way to find, for example all VPs of Marketing in a 50-mile radius who may have graduated from the same school as you did. This is a great tool for prospecting and job search.

Another good practice is to analyze who is following what organizations, schools, or influencers. It can tell you a lot about that person - their hobbies, interests, alumni affiliations, political views, etc. The more you know about the person you are doing business with, the better.

- Search
  - Contacts
    - Tags
  - Groups
  - Companies
- Analyze
  - Followers
  - Similar businesses

As far as your profile, make sure it's as complete as possible. As a rule of thumb, treat it like your public resume online. Use the same rules as for resume writing. Include links to any of your achievements, portfolios, or publications.

First of all, get a professional headshot. A good picture is worth a lot as a first impression. Second, customize your LinkedIn URL for your personal branding. Check out LinkedIn Help on how to do it.

- Complete profile
- Good picture
- Customize your URL
- Build network
  - Start with customers
  - Employees
  - Prospects
  - Use tags
  - Emails
  - Tradeshows
- Share updates on LinkedIn and Tweeter

As far as building a network, start with people you know well to get some practice. Always send thanks for connecting. Reach out on LinkedIn to all your customers, employees, and business associates. Reach out to anyone you have met in a business capacity. Aim for at least 500 connections in the first 6 months. The power of LinkedIn is related to the size of your network.

- Give and take
  - o Recommendations
  - o Introductions
- Don't spam
- No direct sales pitches

Ask for and give recommendations. As long as they are real and sincere, they are very valuable in building your brand.

ALWAYS avoid spam and direct sales pitches. The rules here are identical to any networking group. It takes several months or years to build up trust and credibility.

The immediate value to be gained from LinkedIn is more related to research. You can find a lot of information about people and businesses and you can find out who knows who. But building trust will take some time.

- Triggers giving your permission to reach out to LinkedIn members:
  - o Your profile viewed
  - o Your invitation accepted
  - o Contact's:
    - Promotion
    - Birthday
    - Job change
    - Work anniversary
    - Profile update
    - Mention in the news

Here are triggers giving you permission to reach out to your LinkedIn member.

When your profile is viewed or your invitation is accepted always acknowledge it with a 'Thank you' note and ask how you can be of help. When your contact has a promotion, birthday, job change, work anniversary, profile update or is mentioned in the news it's always a good idea to reach out to them with a 'Congratulation' note.

- Triggers giving your permission to reach out to LinkedIn members:
  - Your publication or post was:
    - Liked
    - Shared
    - Commented on
  - You are invited to a group
  - You are endorsed for a skill
  - Your contact writes a publication

Another trigger to give you permission to reach out to your LinkedIn members is when your publication was liked, shared or commented on. Then the best practice is to thank for those comments. Another best practice is when you're invited to a group or if you're endorsed for a skill and last but not least when your contact writes a publication.

6

TWITTER OVERVIEW

You may think that Twitter is for self-absorbed narcissistic celebrities and their followers only. It indeed started as just a social media platform. However, over time it expanded into the business mainstream.

There were several reasons for that. The first was that celebrities tend to create very large followings and their followers are a very well defined target market for products that are trendy, such as fashion, music, movies, or other entertainment. It was obvious that anybody following and retweeting the Kardashians' posts is in the market for the latest shoes, swimsuits, and fancy accessories.

- Concise nature – 140 characters only
- Short attention span
- No long rants online

The second reason was the concise nature of the posts being limited to only 140 characters. This was a technical limitation when Twitter was being born and it's no longer valid; but, paradoxically, it became its great differentiator. People do not have the attention span for long posts and rants online.

- Started as trivia
- Expanded into the business mainstream

- Anybody following Kardashians is a target for fashion products

The third was that all Twitter posts remain in the public domain for 2 weeks. What this means is that I do not have to be a Kardashian's friend or follower on Twitter to be able to view their posts. This is different from Facebook where I can see only posts created by my Facebook friends. This means that a single post on Twitter can be seen by all 400 million users at the same time (if they choose to view it). Translation – a single post on Twitter has possibly a wider reach than a single Facebook post.

- All tweets are in public domain for 2 weeks
- Do not have to be a Kardashian's friend or follower to view their tweets
- Unlike Facebook where I can see only posts from my friends
- Single tweet has wider reach than a single Facebook post

Twitter then got picked up by journalists who realized the power of its reach. They would post a tweet with a title or synopsis of their article and provide a link to it so the entire column can be read on their website.

Then PR departments picked it up as a great tool to manage public relations. Soon, every CEO was tweeting (or rather their Twitter account was managed in their name by their staff).

Next were consultants who wanted to position themselves as experts on Twitter.

Then every conference and trade show realized that they needed to jump on the bandwagon. The snowballing effect took place, and critical mass was achieved. It was in everyone's interest to use Twitter to spread the word.

Now, every serious opinion leader uses Twitter.

- Journalists picked it up to promote themselves and their publications
- PR departments picked it up as well
- Next were CEOs an consultants
- Conferences/Trade shows
- Now most opinion leaders are on Twitter

Therefore, if I am a salesperson working on a prospective account where the CEO is tweeting, I probably should pay attention to his or her posts. The same is true for my existing key accounts, partners, and competitors.

As we discussed before, I need to pay attention to their Facebook activities for the same reason as well.

- As a salesperson you just need to pay attention to tweets from:
  o Prospects
  o Key accounts
  o Partners
  o Competitors

Twitter remains the least understood in business, especially in the B2B world. It is still perceived as a trivial pursuit by many senior executives.

It may have limited value as an outbound B2B revenue generation channel, but it is invaluable as a sales intelligence and market research tool.

- The least understood in business
- Especially in the B2B world
- Still perceived as a triviality…
- …but invaluable in sales intelligence and market research

Many Twitter users will reveal information that they may not share on LinkedIn or their websites. For example, a CEO may retweet some important information that will never show up on Facebook or a company website.

Think of Twitter as a way of sending a text message that can be read by anyone in the world as long as they have a Twitter account. This is probably the best way to envision Twitter's unique functionality.

- Posting on Twitter but not on LinkedIn or website
- Sending a text message that can be read by anyone in the world with Twitter account

Twitter has become a fierce competitor to news organizations. More and more people learn about critical events from Twitter first. This was true about several terrorist attacks and natural disasters. Journalists cannot be first everywhere, but there are always some spectators with a smartphone and a Twitter account nearby.

Like Facebook, Twitter is instrumental in reputation management. We will show you later on how to set up a system that will listen for negative posts on Twitter.

As of recently, Twitter is being used in both recruitment and job search. Prospective employers as well as headhunters tweet about the availability of jobs.

Similar to all other social media platforms, you can have personal and company accounts; but this requires thoughtful formulation and implementation of a company-wide communication policy. The larger the organization, the more challenging this undertaking will be.

For all B2B companies, we recommend that you may not *need* to tweet, but you should definitely *listen* to tweets coming from your prospects, customers, partners, and competitors. We'll elaborate on this topic later in the section.

- Competitor to news organizations
- Reputation management

- Recruitment
- Personal and company accounts/handles
- May not need to tweet but should listen

7

TWITTER HASHTAGS AND HANDLES

The real challenge with Twitter is how to isolate the relevant posts among billions of tweets.

If we have only 140 characters per tweet how could we do that?

The idea was born to include the subject matter - or a tag - in a body of a tweet itself to address a 140-character limit per tweet.

- Challenge on how to separate the relevant from billions of tweets
- Messages ae limited to 140 characters
- 'Subject matter' or a 'tag' embedded in a tweet and preceded by a # sign
- No spaces in a tag, as spaces count against 140 character limit

To make it distinguishable to both humans and computers a rule was adopted that a subject matter or a tag describing a tweet will be embedded in a tweet itself and preceded by a # sign. There will be no spaces in this 'subject line' as Twitter counts spaces against a 140-character limit.

Therefore, if you wanted to write about your love of milk chocolate and to start a discussion on the subject of this delicious sweet treat, you would create a subject line reading #ilovemilkchocolate. Unlike regular notes, your tweet or post does not have to start with a subject line.

Therefore, your chocolate tweet may look like:

Yesterday I found a great new brand in my corner store #ilovemilkchocolate.

When a traditional reader may be expecting:

I love milk chocolate. Yesterday I found a great new brand in my corner store.

The second message would be easier to understand for humans but much harder for computers, which would not know what part of the post is a subject line.

This requirement to adapt to computer rules is usually very confusing to Twitter beginners. They logically expect a tweet to start with a subject and the subject itself to be spelled with spaces for easy reading.

This confusion leads, in my judgment, to lower adoption of Twitter among more traditional audience who neither appreciate nor understand the perceived awkwardness and inconvenience of such form of communication.

However, once they get used to it, it becomes their second nature like putting a subject line in every email message.

- Hash = hatch = #
- Hatch = parallel lines crossing others
- Hashtag = hatched subject matter
- Expanded to other social media, especially Instagram

By the way, a term 'hash' is derived from a word 'hatch' which denotes a series of **parallel lines** crossing others like in a hatched fence.

Hence, now we have hashtags or 'hatched subject lines' ☺.

Hashtags became quite popular on the other social media platforms and are especially popular on Instagram.

We do not recommend using more than 2 hashtags per tweet just for readability, but there is no limit on the number of hashtags per tweet, other than 140 characters.

Hashtags are also very useful to analyze trends on Twitter and other social media. Computers can easily calculate and group all the unique hashtags and sort the groups high to low with respect to the most popular one in any given timeframe and geography (Twitter posts carry your geographical location if you do not turn this option off on your smartphone).

Geographical analysis of hashtags is how we know that certain topics are trending well in Toronto but not in London or Chicago.

There is one more confusion about hashtags regarding their ownership. In reality no one owns or has rights to any hashtag and anyone can create their own. Just like with subject lines in your email.

However, some hashtags became famous. **#IceBucketChallenge was used over 6 million times in 2014 to promote a cure for** Lou Gehrig's disease by watching celebrities being doused with cold water.

Analysis of all most popular hashtags could be a basis for a great dissertation for PhD candidates in sociology, psychology, political science or media.

- No one owns hashtags
- #IceBucketChallenge – used over 6 million times

Another way to group billions of tweets or Twitter posts is to do it by a user ID.

'Handle' is a Twitter name for your user name or a nickname. User name or handle start with an @ sign. You claim your 'handle' or username when you first open your Twitter account.

To find out handles for people or organizations use Search Twitter dialog box.

Click on Search Twitter and start typing an organization name. Let's say we want to find all handles for Accenture. Larger organizations have multiple Twitter accounts specific to their various departments.

Just typing acc brought up several Accenture Twitter handles. Let's select Accenture Digital. Their specific handle can be found under their logo. It's @AccentureDigi. All Twitter user names or handles start with an @ sign and have no spaces.

This is a similar concept to a hashtag. It makes it easy for computers to search for them and group posts around them, but it is not immediately intuitive to the beginners. Handles are used in a body of a post to mention and/or address a particular user.

- Another way to group tweets
- Handle = Twitter username = nickname
- Username or handle starts with an @ sign

Finally, you can type any keyword in Twitter search box to look for any posts containing that phrase. Let's try 'cute cats'. As expected, we got tweets showing cute kitties.

I'll also discuss special software such as Hootsuite which allows us to group tweets by some logical criteria.

Trade shows create unique hashtags to encourage participants to discuss conference topics while branding their shows.

8

THE ANATOMY OF A SINGLE TWEET

Let's assume that Accenture is a prospect or even an existing client. I will use Twitter to get the latest information on this business.

First we'll find Accenture's Twitter account.

Next, we can examine the main screen for Accenture's Twitter account with all its tweets in the center.

The following tweet caught my attention. Let's examine it.

Want to be more like a #FinTech? Your bank can be fast and nimble with #ValueNetworks. http://bddy.me/2a4aqgr

This tweet is made of regular text plus 2 hashtags and one link to a website.

The first hashtag #FinTech - what is it and what is the significance of it? To find out, we can click on this particular hashtag and examine it in more detail.

It turns out that #FinTech is a tag for professionals who work in technologies for financial companies. This particular group of professionals decided to use this hashtag as a way to brand themselves on Twitter as well as to group all their tweets in one place for reference.

Hashtags are indeed tags preceded by a # sign. They allow us to tag our tweets for themes, topics, or events. Such tagging allows other Twitter users to 'intercept' our tweets and to interact with them by either responding directly or re-tweeting.

Almost all professional conferences come up with a hashtag for themselves for the reasons outlined before. Following is an example of health-related conferences in the U.S. with their respective hashtags.

The second hashtag, #ValueNetworks, is an example of a business concept. I quickly googled it and found the following definition:

A **value network** is a business analysis perspective that describes social and technical resources within and between businesses.

Let's go back to the tweet that caught our attention.

Finally, we have a link at the end of this tweet p://bddy.me/2a4aqgr

It does not look like a typical web address or URL – it's an abbreviated version of a much longer address. Twitter limits the number of characters per tweet to 140. As you can see, after we clicked on this abbreviated but still unique address, it brought us to a standard long URL:

https://www.accenture.com/us-en/insight-banking-reinvented-beyond-value-chains-networks?c=strat_stratsmctwt_10000175&n=smc_0316

This turned out to be an Accenture website page with a white paper on value networks. After we scroll to the bottom of this page, we find two Accenture executives involved in this project.

Both executives have LinkedIn icons displayed next to their names. I will click on the first one and, after scrolling down, I quickly find out that one of my friends is his contact. Depending on the strength of this relationship, I may ask for an introduction.

When I talk to this Accenture manager I will be prepared...

The two hashtags and a white paper provided me with a lot of information. I've learned that value networks and the FinTech conference must be quite important to Steve and Accenture. Otherwise they would not have broadcast it around the world. 'Value network' seems to be a buzzword *du-jour* and the knowledge of this concept may be very helpful during a sales cycle or job interview.

In a nutshell, in less than 10 clicks, we discovered a leading trend for a company we have interest in, found out who else is involved, and learned that we have a friend who can introduce us on LinkedIn.

This is a good example of the very efficient intelligence gathering achieved by combining the powers of Twitter and LinkedIn.

- Two hashtags and a white paper provided a lot of information
- In less than 10 clicks we discovered:
    - Major trends
    - Buzzwords
    - Executives
    - Common friends on LinkedIn

9

COMPOSING TWEETS

In this section we will go over the basics of composing and posting tweets.

Start typing a simple message.

"This is my first tweet."

As you type you will notice that the counter at the bottom went down from 140 to 118. This means that you have 118 characters left to reach the limit of 140 per message.

Next we will try a more complicated message.

Let's say you want to tell the world that you're taking a cool seminar on digital marketing from a certain teacher and you recommend that people visit his website for more information

You may want to type:

"I am learning about cool digital marketing topics by Professor Greg Gutkowski. He recommends visiting this website at https://www.accentur"

Oops! The counter tells me I have no characters left. There is no way to finish this post using the full URL . I've run out of characters.

So let's see how we can squeeze this post into 140 characters without compromising the message itself, and maybe even enhancing it.

Here is an alternative approach using hashtags, handles, and URL shortening:

"I am learning about cool #digitalmarketing topics by @GutkowskiG. He recommends visiting goo.gl/cpwX4p".

First, I used the hashtag #digitalmarketing. I know it is popular because Twitter suggested it when I started typing #digital. This hashtag enhances my message, as it will be easily found by anyone interested in that topic. I saved one space but used one for the hashtag, so in terms of saving characters it's a wash. But my message will reach many more people.

Instead of "Professor Greg Gutkowski" I used his Twitter name or handle, which is @GutkowskiG. This reduced the number characters used to refer to him from 24 to 11 (spaces count as well) thus saving me 13 characters. Twitter also helped me with typing this handle by allowing me to select it from a list of matching handles.

However, we got the biggest character-count savings by shortening the URL to this short one.

To get any URL shortened, go to https://goo.gl/, paste or type the URL and click on shorten URL. Then copy the shorter version and paste it into your Twitter post.

In summary, use as many hashtags as relevant to spread your message, utilize handles to shorten real names, and use the URL shortener to reduce the number of characters in long web addresses.

In general, Twitter posts with no hashtags, handles or links are much less effective in communicating on this social media platform.

Remember that handles and hashtags are clickable when displayed by Twitter users. This translates to more efficient and effective consumption of Twitter content by all participants. They can quickly look you up and see other tweets related to your hashtag by just clicking on them.

10

TWITTER BEST PRACTICES

Let's now talk about Twitter Best Practices.

We recommend that you follow your major customers, prospects, industry leaders, and partners. Active users of Twitter will notice that you follow them and they will appreciate it.

We also recommend that you analyze who they follow. This will tell you who they pay attention to. You may want to check their activities as well.

One of the best practices to get noticed is to retweet their posts to help them spread their messages to your followers. This will be appreciated even more than following. They will know that you are paying very close attention.

- Request to follow major customers, prospects, industry leaders, partners
- Analyze who they follow
- Re-tweet their posts

Keep your tweets short and specific to one topic. You can always include links to more content if you have longer message to convey.

Make sure when tweeting that you put a link to relevant pages on your website whenever you can (use the link shortener). There are two reasons for that. First, you help to bring traffic to that page. The second is that you can find out which tweets were the most effective (or clicked on) from the analysis of your website. Google Analytics will show Twitter as a source of your traffic.

Use visuals in your tweets - add images or video. It will result in higher engagement rates.

Incorporate relevant hashtags, and do not use more than two per tweet. This is a powerful way to expand your reach and get involved in relevant conversations. For example, when tweeting from a trade show or a conference use their hashtag in your tweets. It will help you to connect with other conference participants.

Leverage Hootsuite to manage your Twitter account by creating streams related to various topics. We will cover this in more depth in the Hootsuite chapter.

- Keep it short
- Include links to yoru website
- Use visuals – pictures and videos
- Use relevant hashtags
- Leverage Hootsuite to manage your Twitter

—

11

FEEDLY

Feedly is free software allowing users to easily aggregate a lot of content from around the Internet, organize it, and share it.

It can be used in two major ways:
- as a personal reference for topics of interest, and
- as a source of content to be shared with prospects, customers, and business partners, etc.

Let's imagine that you are looking for a job with Toyota or you want to sell something to Toyota, or Toyota is your major customer. Wouldn't you want to watch for news on Toyota from around the world? You probably would—and should!

When you find an article relevant to your situation, you may want to send it to your prospect, customer, or future employer, thus showing that you are on top of the news and that you really care. This is much better than sending another email asking for a status.

Feedly offers a free account. I suggest you take advantage of it and learn the basic functionality before moving to the PRO version.

Let's say that the particular article caught our attention and we may want to share it. We click on this article to display all the content and after reading it, we decide that indeed we want to share it with one of our prospective customers.

At the top of the article on the left hand side, we see many sharing options: Buffer, email, Twitter, LinkedIn, Hootsuite, and many other.

Let's assume that you know that your prospect is on vacation for the next two weeks and you want to schedule this sharing for later via Hootsuite.

All you have to do is to click on the Hootsuite icon and schedule a post for two weeks later.

You can also share it on LinkedIn and Twitter.

In summary, I find Feedly to be a great aggregator of news I care about. It's all in one place, with easy navigation. Even more important, sharing content is very easy and all major platforms are supported, including Hootsuite and Evernote.

It is a great source for news as well as for the curation of content that you can share with prospective or existing customers or business partners.

12

GOOGLE ALERTS

Google Alerts are great way to monitor any phrase or name on the Internet. Any website accessible to Google could be a source of information. Google alerts is another way to find a relevant content that may be shared in the sales process. It's also a great source for competitive information.

I recommend that you create a separate Google email account just for this function. I will show you later how you can integrate it with Hootsuite dashboard.

Let me show you how it works.

You will type https://www.google.com/alerts in your browser to find Google alerts website. This brings up an extremely easy interface.

I'll create an alert about BMW. I'll type in "BMW" in the "Create an alert about" box. Then click "Create Alert". My alert on "BMW" has been created. To check the content of the alerts just scroll down. All this content will be pushed to my Gmail account associated with this alert.

I expect I will already find these two alerts in my email box.

I would recommend that you create as many alerts as reasonable. Just create about 10 for your major accounts and then expand based on your experience. These alerts can be brought directly to our dashboard. I'll talk about this some more when we cover Hootsuite.

As you can see, the alerts can be easily shared on other social media.

Google Alerts is indeed a simple and very powerful intelligence system.

- Another way to find content to be shared
- Set up a separate gmail account
- Set up alerts
- Feed to Hootsuite stream

13

EVERNOTE

Evernote is a cloud-based note-taking application. This means that you can add, read, and manage all your notes whether you're working on a desktop, laptop, smartphone, or tablet. All the content created on any of these devices will be accessible and editable on the others, as all the content is stored and synced in one location somewhere in the cloud.

When you start your Evernote work on your desktop in your office and you need to revise it while waiting at the airport, you can do it with ease. If you start your note on your iPhone while waiting in a coffee shop, you can finish it on your laptop when you get back to the office.

Evernote is integrated with Feedly and Hootsuite, and allows sharing on major social media platforms. In addition, Evernote can be configured to support teams of professionals collaborating on common projects.

It is easy to use, very powerful, and the basic version is free.

We have the full-blown functionality of a word processor at our disposal. We can also drag images directly to our note.

Notes can be organized into multiple Notebooks. Notes can also be organized by Tags. Clicking on the Tag icon on our menu will bring up all our tags organized alphabetically. As you can guess, clicking on a tag will bring up the corresponding notes. You can easily create your own tags.

We can also share notes on different social media platforms as well as Hootsuite.

One of the handiest features is an Evernote extension on my browser. Let's say I want to look up a particular IBM website. After I locate it, I can click on the Evernote extension in my browser and bring this content directly to my notes. After clicking on the Evernote icon extension, a dialog box pops up and asks me what existing notebook I want to save this note to and what tag I want to assign to it. I will select a Technology tag and save that page.

When we go back to Evernote and look up my notes, we will notice that, 2 minutes ago, this note showed up here. The whole page from the IBM website was saved as a note—and it can even be edited!

This is a very handy way to store content coming directly from websites.

Evernote allows for easy search of text inside notes. We just click on the magnifying glass icon on the menu and start searching. We can also limit a search to a single notebook.

In summary, Evernote is a very easy yet very powerful note-taking app. The ease of creating, tagging, and sharing combined with the synchronization of content creation on multiple devices such as browsers, Android and iOS devices makes it a very compelling tool to organize our busy professional lives.

Extensive note taking and good organization of content is very important in social selling as you need to share a lot of relevant information with many different recipients. It is great for storing and finding proposals, documentation, reference materials, manuals in text or PDF formats.

- Archive content
- Annotate
- Take notes
- Share with your team
- Share socially

14

HOOTSUITE

Hootsuite was designed to manage multiple social media accounts for large companies where numerous individuals are involved in creation and posting of the content. Imagine a global company with a large marketing team needing to coordinate all the social media posts in various countries around the world while introducing a new product globally.

However, Hootsuite is also perfect to monitor social media to gather competitive information, do market research, or generate sales leads.

Let's take a look at this powerful system. The software is designed to be very simple to use. The basic package is free. The interface is made up of 'streams' of posts from various social media platforms.

On one screen, we can display the latest posts from Facebook, Twitter, YouTube, LinkedIn, Instagram, Gmail and many others.

We can even bring our Evernotes in here as well. They are all live, so if I click on one, I can display the entire content of that note.

A great time saver is that we can interact with all these posts directly from Hootsuite here. We can add comments to Facebook. We can retweet, "like" on LinkedIn, post from Pinterest, archive gmails, share Evernotes on Twitter, and add comments on YouTube. All the functionality of social media is available directly from this dashboard without having to log in and out of multiple social media accounts.

Very powerful indeed. In one interface or dashboard we can display information from various sources, monitor our own social media accounts, interact, share, and comment.

Let's say we want to display all the latest tweets about our competition. Let's assume that we compete with ADT Security. We can learn a lot by examining tweets mentioning ADT.

For example, we can see somebody is complaining:

"If you're current @ADT customer get out when you can. Service is terrible and no concern over predatory sales."

If you are competing with ADT, this is extremely valuable information about their poor quality of their service.

This is a perfect example of the reputation management challenges that we talked about before.

In total, you can monitor and interact with 200 social media entities from one simple interface. That is very powerful.

And we have not talked yet about the ability of Hootsuite to schedule your posts, collaborate with your social media team, and setting the process whereby the content written by junior staff members can be queued up for the review/approval by more senior members before the actual posting takes place. Social media are too important to publish content without quality control!

As I mentioned, the basic Hootsuite package is free. It allows you to connect to 3 social media accounts. If you want to use Hootsuite with more than 3 social media platforms, the next level of membership is about $10 month.

15

HOOTSUITE BEST PRACTICES

The best Hootsuite practice is to create separate tabs for

- Competitors
- Prospects
- Products
- Customers
- Trade Shows and Key Industry Magazines
- Thought leaders

This will help you to organize tweets, emails, YouTube videos, etc. efficiently, which will save time otherwise spent on too much searching around. You'll be surprised how much information you can find that you may not have been aware of before, that may be very helpful in the sales process.

You may not find direct leads there, but you can find information that will help you better qualify prospects, speed up the sales process, or close a sale.

Fill out each tab with streams of tweets that are addressed to, coming from, or mention a particular company. You will then have a very comprehensive view of all aspects of their Twitter presence.

Many Twitter users will reveal information that they may not share on LinkedIn or their websites. For example, a CEO may retweet some important information that will never show up on Facebook or a company website.

Configure Hootsuite to your liking. There is no bad way of doing it. It's very individual. Give yourself about 4 weeks of learning how others are using social media, who are very active, and how frequently they post. If your major prospect is tweeting twice a day, you may need to pay attention to it quite frequently.

We advise engaging gradually. Commenting and re-tweeting is a good start. It let's your customers or prospects know that you are paying attention and helping them spread their message.

Post curated content you found with Feedly or gmail only if it is relevant to the sales cycle or customer service. Do not post trivia – keep it strictly professional.

The best practice is to post your own content, but few of us have time to be a writer on top of our daily responsibilities.

Visit your Hootsuite dashboard for about 10 minutes daily. The idea is not to spend too much time there, but to spend enough time to catch the 'buying signals'.

Hootsuite allows you to schedule your posts for any date in the future. This is very handy for several reasons. For example, you may know that your prospect is on vacation and there is no way they can see your post before they return. You may have a lot of relevant content, but you don't want to share it all at the same time – you can spread it over time. And last but not least, you can plan your communication so you don't have to do it under the duress of daily chores.

Social selling is a term describing processes and tools to leverage social media platforms primarily in B2B sales and marketing. It is another tool in your sales toolbox, but does not replace the traditional sales training and methods. It enhances them.

In this section we concentrated on how to use social media to discover, explore, and learn as much as we can about our prospective and existing customers, business partners, and competitors. We did not talk much about how social media supports traditional marketing – this could be a separate book by itself.

We concentrated on listening and research. However, we discussed at length on how to engage in social media conversations on Twitter and LinkedIn and how to add value in a sales cycle by providing timely and relevant information to all stakeholders.

A big part of effective engagement is the professional image we project with our profiles. We discussed how to look professional on various social media platforms.

In sales, information is power and we taught you how to sift for information nuggets in a social media goldmine using Hootsuite Dashboard.

Twitter and LinkedIn are the two most important social media for social selling. Twitter's intimacy and immediacy combined with the live resumes and networking capabilities of LinkedIn provide a lot of very useful information.

More good information should help you to find and close more deals.

16

EMAIL

Email is an indispensable and powerful sales tool. We have discussed the features and functions of the temporary email system in Chapter 4.9 Part II. In the context of sales, email is usually integrated with CRM systems to send, respond, and track activities tied to each of our customers in one convenient place. This saves a lot of time spent on searching for relevant emails in extensive archives.

17

CUSTOMER RELATIONSHIP MANAGEMENT (CRM)

Marketing Automation, and Customer Experience

CRM is a software system used to manage a company's interactions with current and potential customers. The ultimate goal is to drive sales and increase customer retention and profits.

CRMs are designed to collect customer data from all communication channels including websites, telephone calls, email, chatbots, text, and social media.

Such data allows for a better understanding of customer needs. It is the basis for customer segmentation and the subsequent customization and personalization of communication and services.

If you have a sales team calling on prospects, they are probably utilizing some form of tracking software, even if it's an Excel spreadsheet.

From the sales perspective, we need to track the sales process from the initial contact through sale presentations, proposal submissions, and final negotiations. The longer the sales cycle, and the more decision makers involved, the greater the need for tracking.

- 12+ month sales cycle

- Multiple players
  - Own support
  - Selection committee
- Request for proposal (RFP)
- From VP to admin person
- Constant communication and coordination

All in One

The only way to do it effectively is to have a system that records all these interactions in one place, each with a time stamp.

There are several systems on the market to support such complex undertakings. They are called CRM for Customer Relationship Management—a little misnomer as we are managing a prospect who is not yet a customer.

Every phone call and every email regarding this sale is automatically logged. Dialing a phone number automatically logs the call timing and duration. A sales rep fills out other information, such as specifics on the next steps.

- One place
- Time stamp on all interactions
- Customer Relationship Management systems
- Every interaction logged either manually or automatically
  - Call
  - Email/document sent
  - Visit
  - Conversation

Prospect and Competitive Analysis

The sales cycle starts with careful analysis of the social media profiles and posts of all 10 selection committee members. The sales rep needs access to

LinkedIn, Twitter, Facebook, and possibly Pinterest and Instagram. The analysis will reveal the members' professional and personal backgrounds, schools they went to, as well as their hobbies, interests, the publications they read, etc. LinkedIn would reveal that our rep's best buddy went to school with the VP. A separate entry will be made in the CRM for each of the committee members. Each one will have automatic look-up of their social media profile. A good sales rep will look for any common touch points to build rapport.

Next is a competitive analysis. What do we know about the competition, their products? Social media as well as analysis of the competition's websites will provide a lot of useful information. Maybe there are a lot of complaints on Twitter about the competitive products. Maybe a competitor is experiencing serious financial problems. You need to examine recent articles (via subscription to sites such as Feedly or Scoop.it) and set up Google alerts. A separate entry will be created in CRM for each competitor. Again, such information may mean the difference between winning or losing a multimillion dollar sale.

- Social media
    - Profiles (personal and corporate)
    - Tweets, posts, discussions
- Websites
- Articles
- Google alerts

Mundane Paperwork and Documentation

Following that, there will be your response to the RFP. On your side, you will need input from corporate, your manager, and the cooperation of an admin to put it all together and FedEx it to the client. How are you going to track all these interactions and their timing? CRM and document management systems come to the rescue. All revisions and communication steps will be logged with exact time stamps.

- Response to RFP
- Document management / version management

- Responding to additional questions

- Ongoing Interactions

Then, a rep will be alerted automatically by CRM that there were a lot of searches on the corporate website from the prospective customer site (this can be tracked by IP address). A more detailed analysis shows that the most and the longest visits were on pages devoted to product specs and testimonials. So far so good.

Next, for some unexplained reason, things go silent for 2 months. None of the members responded to phone calls or opened any email from our sales rep (email systems allow for tracking of opened emails). This is not a good sign. Something serious must be going on at the prospective customer. Our rep finds relevant articles on the prospect's business and emails them to maintain visibility without looking desperate.

Finally, a single simple tweet from the CEO of the prospective company announces a major acquisition.

So it's reasonable to expect that our sale got delayed due to that event and our sales cycle is still alive.

During these ups and downs, the sales manager and his boss are very interested in the status. No problem; they can log in to the CRM and get an update anytime they want.

Finally, our rep gets invited back for the negotiations. They take about 3 tense weeks and everyone wants a daily status update.

After 3 weeks, the agreement is signed. At year end, a nice bonus arrives for everyone involved. The end of a story—or is it?

A new phase has just been born and it's called....customer service

Visits to your website

- Prospect goes silent
- Managing your management's expectations
- Monitoring prospect's activities
- Contract finally signed!

Customer Service

Using the same CRM, all interactions with the new customer are logged in, this time by customer service reps. Any implementation hiccups, complaints, or delays are very well known to our rep who is still in charge of managing the overall relationship. New members of the customer's organization are added to CRM. Our sales rep watches every step of implementation and checks with his primary contact to see if the new customer is satisfied. Everything is going relatively smoothly and the new customer brags on social media that they got a great deal. The contract gets renewed for another year.

Our rep learns that the new customer contemplates rolling out the new product to all subsidiaries. A very enticing proposal with a nice discount is proposed. In March of the following year, the customer puts in an order five times as big as the original one.

- After the sale need to manage implementation
- Switching to customer service mode
- Managing hiccups, complaints and delays
- Upselling
- Hard to manage such complexity without many digital tools

In summary, CRM facilitated successful management of multi-step, multi-person, multi-organization, multi-state sales process that involved competitive research, analysis of social media and web traffic, multiple email interactions, in-person visits, call tracking, internal reporting and communication, and RFP generation—all from a single platform. It made the whole team more productive, better informed, and satisfied. It flagged the opportunity for a big upsell and made the customer very happy (not to mention the sales rep's manager—and the rep, too).

In the past it was rather hard to manage such a process using separate Outlook emails, Excel spreadsheets, Word documents, tons of paper, and constant interruptions from nervous managers seeking updates. A lot of balls were dropped and a lot of things fell through the cracks.

The integration of CRMs with social media, web visit analysis, document management, email campaigns, and their tracking has a profound positive impact on complex sales processes.

The functionalities we have just described are almost identical to digital marketing activities. And indeed, many CRM vendors are adding features to their systems that blend digital marketing functions such as web analytics, email, and social media management with existing tracking and document management capabilities.

Examples of such integrated systems include HubSpot and SharpSpring. To differentiate themselves from CRM vendors they call themselves Marketing Automation platforms, but they include CRM. No wonder this could be a little confusing.

Speaking of confusion and new terms—the latest buzzword is 'Customer Experience'. The idea is that we need to manage all aspects of interactions with our customers, including the entire journey from promotion, evaluation, selection, and buying to using our products, and we need to manage it in real time and digital space.

Thus, the term 'bricks and clicks' was born to reflect the need to manage customer interaction in physical brick-and-mortar stores as well as online.

Though I am not a big fan of buzzwords, I admit I like this term because it indeed covers all aspects of customer relationships with any company. Today, it is impossible to improve the customer experience without some kind of CRM system.

A systematic way to record and analyze all customer interactions in one software system yields the following four big-picture benefits in addition to allowing for tactical sales management:

1. Enhance customer services: in general, customers always have some questions, concerns, or requests. CRM provides a way to collect, allocate, and manage requests made by customers.

2. Increased one-on-one service: personalizing customer service or one-on-one service can only happen with a broad understanding of the customers' preferences, requirements, and demands.

3. Customer segmentation: CRM is used to categorize customers into groups based on similar aspects such as industry, job, or some other characteristic. Companies can customize their products or services based on such segmentation to maintain customer interests.

4. Time savings: CRM will let companies interact with customers more frequently, by personalized messaging and communication that can be produced rapidly and matched on a timely basis.

18

DIGITAL SALES SUMMARY

The principles of selling have not changed in ages and will not change anytime soon. You always need to understand consumers' needs, timing, and ability to pay for whatever they are buying. Everything else being equal, you need to find customers, articulate your message, and communicate why buying from you is to their advantage.

What is new is the number of prospective customers you can serve and the effectiveness of doing so. When dealing with a very large number of customers who have a wide variety of needs, budgets, and timeframes, it is almost impossible to do it all the old-fashioned way of keeping track of all interactions in your head or on paper or even in separate Excel files and email accounts.

In sales, information is power. But only if it's easily collected, found, shared, and used. Given the realities of connected customers who have a lot of information and the freedom to do business with whomever they want, it is unlikely that success will come without a systematic way to collect the relevant information. However, the cost of information collection cannot exceed the benefit; hence, the more information we can collect automatically, the better the result.

Collection is not enough if the collected information is not easily accessible, shareable, and easy to analyze. Sales people need to be selling and not acting like data entry clerks or data scientists. Therefore, the ease of use of systems providing sales information to sales professionals is of utmost importance.

On the other hand, successful sales people have no choice but to keep learning new digital tools and techniques to be more effective and efficient. For example, if a customer uses Snapchat or Instagram or WhatsApp, a salesperson better learn how to leverage it. :-)

PART IV

CUSTOMER EXPERINCE
Clicks and Bricks

1

INTRODUCTION

Let's talk about the recent monumental power shift toward consumers and away from businesses.

In the past, you had to set aside time for shopping and physically go to a store. With limited hours in a day, you could do only so much research. Your options for price comparison were limited. In most states, for example, car dealers lobbied for legislation to stay closed on Sundays, so you had even less time for comparison shopping.

Yes, there were catalog-based mail order firms like Sears, but the selection was rather limited by today's standards. There was the *Consumer Report* monthly paper magazine, but it cost money and did not cover many items that may have been less popular.

There was no public forum to log complaints. There was the Better Business Bureau, but who would bother to go there or call after a bad experience while shopping for a pair of inexpensive T-shirts?

2

CONNECTED CUSTOMER

Enter the Internet and instant free access to all possible products and their prices. Consumers started sharing comments and opinions on products and services on social media using desktop computers.

This put tremendous pressure on B2C (Business to Consumer) businesses. All pricing and product specs, as well as negative and positive opinions, were out in the open.

Next, we witnessed the proliferation of smartphones. Customers carrying smartphones were much more likely to tweet an angry opinion right on the spot as opposed to going home and having to do it on desktops after they had a chance to cool off. The feedback loop became instantaneous.

Amazon was the first to popularize the 5-star rating system for books purchased on their site. This was followed by Apple with 5-star ratings for iPhone apps. Both companies killed the proverbial two birds with one stone. They provided a valuable feedback mechanism to customers and simultaneously a tool to evaluate their suppliers.

Next came Google and Yelp using the by then familiar 5-star system for the real time evaluation of local businesses such as restaurants, roofers, dentists, physicians, etc.

As a result, consumers got used to rating almost anything. This put businesses that had a lot of reviews with an average below 3 stars in real jeopardy.

Consumers simply got spoiled with their power and with the ease of feedback. Therefore, today's customer service needs to be as easy to reach as possible and extremely responsive. In the age of Twitter, few customers will wait 24 hours for an answer. Easy-to-use interfaces on mobile phones, real-time chats, and Twitter support are becoming minimum requirements.

3

REPUTATION MANAGEMENT

Reputation management is a subset of PR and involves the management of testimonials, evaluations, and opinions made on social media or websites and directly related to the quality of products and services offered by the organization. The impact of having poor reviews can be huge, especially if it is not quickly and immediately addressed. On the other hand, the value of good reviews
cannot be overestimated.

A best practice of reputation management for business is to address any complaints directly and publically online as quickly as possible by asking for a live conversation to understand and possibly remedy the situation. For that, you need
to be able to monitor all negative comments that may show up on your social
media accounts as well as public posts on Twitter or Yelp and be alerted in real
time. There are tools on the market to set up such alerts.

Another good practice is to proactively solicit good reviews from satisfied customers and post them on your website and social media accounts. This is a
very good strategy to counter any negative reviews, which can never be avoided
but can be minimized and marginalized.

Reputation management can also involve managing your personal information on
social media, especially if your past posts no longer project the desired image.
This is a widespread problem with the younger audience who, in the past,
may have posted juvenile content that is now visible to potential hiring
managers. However, the same problem may be faced by any member of senior management who wishes to suppress any negative comments on their troubles past or present.

One strategy is to remove links to the undesirable content (which could be time consuming and/or impossible)Another strategy is
to counter the negatives with a highly professional profile on LinkedIn and Facebook as well as the personal website, demonstrating a consistent message.

Keeping Honest

On balance, the shift of power to consumers is very good for both society and the economy. Businesses were forced to be more transparent, less arrogant (think car salesmen), more responsive, and more price sensitive. The fly-by-night operators get slowly weeded out. The best establishments stay in business and remain profitable by providing quality products and services. This is one of the best examples of the virtue of transparency brought about by digital technologies.

The only businesses that escaped this scrutiny are those who enjoy a monopoly and have little incentive to improve. Nevertheless, the overall increase in business service standards puts a lot of pressure on non-competitive services as well.

Keep It Simple

Amazon's Dash Button is a perfect example of simplicity in reordering. Now you can get your detergent with one push of a physical Wi-Fi enabled button stuck with adhesive to your washing machine. You don't even have to go find your smartphone! Better yet, just say, "Alexa! I need a box of Tide."

Such enhanced customer service is now referred to as the 'customer experience'. It includes the traditional functions plus esthetics and simplicity in the service interaction. Everything being equal, a business with an ugly and hard to navigate customer support interface will lose to a competitor who put a lot of thought into making the interaction as easy and appealing as possible.

Customer experience blends digital and physical worlds, and it is a very exciting and growing phenomenon where we see a lot of activity and creativity.

Imagine waiting for service at a car repair shop in a crowded, poorly ventilated, and poorly lit room with drab, worn out furniture, a loud TV, stale coffee, and no Wi-Fi. Contrast this with surroundings in your favorite high-end restaurant... The idea is to have a positive impact on all your senses; sight, hearing, touch, taste, and smell.

A good customer experience is the ease of returning a rental car where an agent checks you out with a handheld digital device without having to visit and wait at the counter. Managing customer expectations also falls into this category.

A great example here is a progress bar providing the status of your Domino's pizza when you order it online. You know when they put your pizza in the oven and took it out, and when the driver left the store. Another great example is FedEx's tracking number emailed to you when your order leaves the dock so you know when to expect delivery. You can track the status of Christmas gift arrivals just before December 25th.

J.D. Power has long been known for rating the quality of cars. Now they provide 5 level ratings by surveying customer satisfaction with the quality of electronics, financial services, healthcare, insurance, retail, travel, and even sports. With sports, they measure fans' satisfaction with ticketing, arriving at the gate, security, ushers, seating, food, beverage, souvenirs, and how easy it was to leave a game.

Royal Treatment

The term 'Customer Experience' blends a lot of familiar concepts, such as:

- convenience (easy to find, park, try & test the product, return, contact, etc.)
- good quality
- personalization
- exclusivity
- ambiance (store or location condition, impression, lighting, character, atmosphere, and even climate control)
- pleasant, professional, and competent personnel
- fast service
- fair price/value
- seamless checkout/payment
- functional, minimal, and esthetic packaging
- efficient delivery
- overall satisfaction

Please note that this does NOT mean low prices. Actually, the better the customer experience, the less need to keep prices low and the better the chances for profitability.

4

CLICKS AND BRICKS

Also, it is worth noting that all the above mentioned attributes span brick-and-mortar as well as online shopping experiences. Thus, customer experience is a blend of digital and physical experiences.

As we discussed before, customers today interact with businesses simultaneously on many channels; in person, via website, smartphone app, phone, text, email, or even traditional mail.

Customers purchase products that may be physical in nature, such as clothing or food, or purely digital, such as movies and songs. Or they buy hybrid products such as smartphones, game consoles, laptops, smart TVs, etc.

Extending and sustaining superior customer experience also blends digital and physical worlds. A great example is a well-designed smartphone app to check into and order room service in a very nice hotel. The same app will also open the room door, let you book a spa, and bill you seamlessly and automatically.

Easier Said Than Done

Extending and supporting such experience requires a well thought out digital and business strategy. Actually, it is getting harder and harder to distinguish one from the other. Technology drives new possibilities in the traditional physical world, as illustrated with the hotel example. Poor or spotty Wi-Fi coverage is not acceptable in a luxury hotel. On the other hand, the best Wi-Fi connectivity will not assure a customer's satisfaction when faced with dirty bedding, rude room service, and substandard food.

As the population grows more affluent, it expects more pampering from all retailers. This in turn raises the bar of expectations with respect to level of service in business-to-business or consumer-to-government transactions. Thus, the need to provide the best possible customer experience forces everyone to increase the level of service regardless of the type of industry or the size of the business.

Relentless Competitive Pressure

The winners are customers, but this trend to keep spoiling them cannot be supported in traditional ways. Hence, the pressure by all businesses to leverage digital technologies to keep up with the competition. This is one of the major drivers of the digital transformation in businesses; i.e., having to constantly invent and/or catch up with new ways to attract and retain customers who are only going to be more and more demanding.

The good news for businesses is that a lot of these customer service related ideas, technologies, and processes are very similar, regardless of the type of business, size, and industry. Thus, all businesses can be inspired by studying other industries which, in the past, would not make sense to compare with. Case in point: chatbot support by smartphone can be used by any business of any size in any industry. The same goes for a good quality website integrated with a customer database that is itself integrated with smart email marketing and a social media management system. So, a small local coffee shop stands to learn how to treat customers from a global manufacturing conglomerate and vice versa.

Frequently, when we think about customers, a retail experience comes to mind; i.e., I've entered a store so I am a customer. However, a teacher commuting to school in the morning is a customer of the school district (not just an employee), publishers (teachers decide on book adoptions), the local transportation system (they use the roads that better be well maintained), and a local coffee shop (assuming they enjoy a morning shot of caffeine). At the same time, teachers are suppliers to students, parents, school districts, the community, and their own family.

Thus, in our lives, we are both customers and suppliers. Simultaneously, we wear the many hats of customers and suppliers every day.

These multiple roles expose us to various customer experiences and raise the overall bar of excellence. It is perplexing and thought provoking to consider why we would be treated like kings or queens by one establishment and as a pariah by another in a span of just a few hours. <u>We all want to be treated royally all the time.</u> And this is one of the major drivers of digital transformation; i.e., increasing affluence and the expectations that come with it.

5

TECHNOLOGICAL COMPLEXITY

Let's list all the technologies typically involved in creating a superior customer experience. We will start our list with promotions and finish with counting profits coming from a customer. After all, we are supposed to service customers while making money!

The following table illustrates typical functions of the customer experience in the first column, and the supporting technology in the second.

Function	System
Social media promotions	Facebook (1), Twitter (2), Instagram (3), etc.
Online ads	AdWords (4) and/or Facebook Ads (5)
Email	Email system (6) such as Constant Contact or MailChimp
Visits to a website	Google Analytics (7)

Forms filled out on website	Google Analytics
Conversation via chatbots	Chatbot technologies (8)
Number of phone calls about products/returns	Call Center (9)
Number of online sales/returns	Google Analytics
Number of in-store sales	Point of Sale Systems (10)
Number of visits to a store	A door-mounted reader at a store (11)
Number of sales associates or support people	HR system (12)
Profit by customer	Accounting system (13)

As illustrated above, one needs to leverage some 10 to 13 separate systems to provide superior customer service without giving away the farm. No wonder it is so hard to implement! In addition, existing technologies are constantly changing and new technologies such as Alexa and chatbots are appearing, seemingly out of nowhere.

6

CUSTOMER EXPERIENCE SUMMARY

In reality, in today's world, customer experience is marketing and marketing is customer experience. It is impossible and impractical to separate them.

The 4 Ps of marketing–price, promotion, place, and product—are all impacted by digital technologies. Prices can be adjusted in real time online based on algorithms (just like airline tickets); promotions are shifted heavily to the Internet and smartphones; place is both online and in-store simultaneously; and product can be easily customized based on customer specifications (embroidered apparel, or custom 3D-printed hearing aids).

As societies become more affluent, their members expect to be pampered and spoiled. Their expectations are always adjusted upward by the most recent best customer experience. This creates relentless pressure to keep up for all businesses large and small, regardless of industry.

The clicks and bricks phenomenon makes delivering such an experience even more challenging for most businesses. Most have no choice but to raise the bar on their own capabilities in this arena or risk being rendered irrelevant. At the same time, most lack the sufficient experience, skills, and talent to consistently deliver an exceptional level of service.

Which brings us to the next section on talent management...

PART V
TALET MANAGEMENT

1

INTRODUCTION

As discussed in the previous section, most businesses do not have enough employees with the relevant experience to provide a superior customer experience. They are not alone. The most serious challenge is the lack of sufficient digital and analytical skills in the U.S. labor force.

This problem is not going to be solved anytime soon due to the neck-breaking advancements in digital technologies that leave colleges behind. They can't adjust curricula fast enough. The burden of digital professional development will be shifting to businesses themselves.

According to McKinsey & Company, educational gaps like the digital skills gap, "impose on the United States the economic equivalent of a permanent national recession."

According to a Harris poll[5], almost 1 in 3 U.S. workers say they simply are not proficient in using the technology tools they need at work. What's more, only 1 in 10 American workers say they have mastered these tools.

From the same Harris poll: "Among workers we spoke to who use customer relationship management tools like Salesforce.com, 40 percent say they are not proficient with this technology. Over a third (35%) of workers using Hootsuite, a popular social media management tool, say they are not proficient at using it properly and only 11 percent consider themselves an expert."

2

CANDIDATE AND EMPLOYEE EXPERIENCE

In the face of a talent shortage, companies will have to compete for the best employees with the voracity they apply to competing for new customers.

The good news is that similar processes and digital technologies can be used for these challenging tasks.

To attract the top talent, companies will have to show a great web presence, pay attention to online reviews and reputation management, and pamper job candidates with ease of finding, applying, and onboarding. Thus, they can use the same techniques they already employ with respect to customers.

The only practical difference is that Applicant Tracking Systems are used instead of Point of Sale systems.

Unfortunately, the remaining 10 or so separate systems (social media, websites, Google Analytics, email, chatbots, text, call center, etc.) are still involved. However, the skills needed to manage them for marketing can be deployed for talent management as well.

The task of managing applicant flow through the hiring process is relatively easy to automate and analyze. There are several good software packages on the market that already do that.

The greater challenge lies in digitizing the process of identifying the always-changing set of relevant skills and identifying the right talents, so as to attract the best candidates and retain them.

In order to accomplish such an ambitious task, HR departments will have to better understand the digital transformation in the context of their own business. Otherwise, it will be hard to assess the skills to be attracted and nourished without broad knowledge of internal processes, products, services, and markets.

If it is true that employees are the company's greatest asset, then we will have to treat employees with the same reverence as we extend to our most valuable customers. Otherwise, unhappy with their 'internal customer experience', they will walk into the waiting arms of the competition or start a competing business. So, everything we discussed with respect to 'customer experience' is also relevant to the employee experience.

Thus, we need to rethink how we even list our jobs and how to facilitate the best match between our needs and candidate characteristics and preferences. Making such a match on keywords on resumes may not be sufficient anymore. Today, on average, recruiters spend only 8 seconds per resume, fetched for them by a keyword matching algorithm. It does not seem like an effective way to source the best talent.

Assess For Success

In the near future, assessing skills in 8 seconds and making a match between a vague job description and a vague resume is not going to be sufficient. Moreover, we need to assess candidates' values, interests, motivations, communication styles, hobbies, and preferences.

This cannot be done by a simple match of keywords between the job description and a resume. Nor can it be done effectively on a large scale via personal interviews. First, it would be too time consuming. Second, we would need for every interviewer to have PhD-level knowledge about the human psyche.

The answer is to include in-depth psychological and skill assessment on each candidate and then match them to available opportunities that are described in specific terms. Easier said than done; however, digital technologies come to the rescue again.

There a several reputable vendors offering online tools for comprehensive and reliable psychological and skills assessments. The trick is to take their output and match it with a well written job description that includes relevant psychological, technical, and physical requirements.

The same assessment technologies can be used on an ongoing basis as skills, jobs, and interests change over time.

Then, it becomes a technical problem that can be solved with technology. However, no technology will solve this problem if the right skills, aptitudes, and attitudes are not identified on both sides of the equation.

The same assessment technologies also become a great way to identify and match professional development training and resources.

The potential for benefits of better employee-employer match-making are enormous and numerous:

- Lower cost of hiring
- Lower cost of on-boarding
- Lower cost of training
- Lower cost of retaining
- Better education
- Better skills
- Higher motivation
- Higher performance
- Higher retention
- Desirable workplace

- 5 Stars on Glassdoor.com (making attracting top talent even easier)

3
LIFETIME LEARNING
Professional Development

As discussed in the previous section, most businesses do not have enough employees with the relevant experience to provide a superior customer experience. They are not alone. The most serious challenge is the lack of sufficient digital and analytical skills in the U.S. labor force.

This problem is not going to be solved anytime soon due to the neckbreaking advancements in digital technologies that leave colleges behind. They can't adjust curricula fast enough. The burden of digital professional development will be shifting to businesses themselves.

Attracting Top Talent

In the face of a talent shortage, companies will have to compete for the best employees with the voracity they apply to competing for new customers.

The good news is that similar processes and digital technologies can be used for these challenging tasks.

To attract the top talent, companies will have to show a great web presence, pay attention to online reviews and reputation management, and pamper job candidates with ease of finding, applying, and onboarding. Thus, they can use the same techniques they already employ with respect to customers.

The only practical difference is that Applicant Tracking Systems are used instead of Point of Sale systems.

Unfortunately, the remaining 10 or so separate systems (social media, websites, Google Analytics, email, chatbots, text, call center, etc.) are still involved. However, the skills needed to manage them for marketing can be deployed for talent management as well.

Learning Managements Systems can measure the number and type of courses taken, time on task, and completion rates, and thus try to understand the relationship between the amount and type of training offered and expected business outcomes.

However, for most organizations it's rather hard to measure the effectiveness of professional development despite the considerable effort tied to this activity.

FINAL THOUGHTS

Digital Marketing, SEO, PPC, Social Media, CRM, Marketing Automation, Customer Experience, Analytics, Talent Management, Digital Skills Gap - we covered a lot of concepts in this book.

As we discussed, every business of any size in any industry needs to pay attention and leverage these tools, techniques, and best practices.

The good news is that regardless of the size and type of business, best practices can be shared and serve as an inspiration and/or benchmark for another. For example, every business needs to look for customers and employees online. Not all the customers and not all the employees are going to be sourced online, but all of them will be heavily influenced by how you treat them digitally in the process of becoming and staying one.

Thus, becoming familiar and comfortable with the feasibility of digital marketing, digital sales, digital customer experience, and digital talent management will enhance your executive skills and make them portable between jobs and industries.

From the managerial perspective, the single largest benefit of digital technologies is that every detailed step of every process can be time-stamped and record the names of the parties to each transaction. This provides tremendous opportunities to identify what works and what doesn't and to act proactively at the time the process is in jeopardy, instead of analyzing it months later without knowing who was even involved.

From the marketing perspective, knowledge of these digital feasibilities will allow you to design creative new 'click & brick' products and services. This will help you compete in the global economy.

If you combine these skills with a lifetime of learning, you will join an elite corps of executives who can manage complex businesses and enjoy a rewarding career of winning rather than catching up.

In an upcoming book titled *Measurement Revolution*, I discuss in more depth the best practices of analyzing your business in the context of voluminous data being generated by all the processes described here.

Connect with me on LinkedIn and share your thoughts.

https://www.linkedin.com/in/greggutkowski

ABOUT THE AUTHOR

Greg Gutkowski, Digital Strategist & Bestselling Author has over 20 years of multidisciplinary global business experience spanning marketing, sales, and IT management, as well as Internet software development, Internet of Things, advanced data analytics, and journalism. Greg has earned the following advanced degrees: MBA in IT Management, MS in Economics, MS in Journalism.

He currently runs the business analytics software company 3CLICKS.US and teaches digital strategies at the University of North Florida Coggin College of Business.

Greg has worked over the years with customers from various industries. He has helped, among others: Allstate, American Express, Aon/Hewitt, AT Kearney, AT&T, Blue Cross Blue Shield of Illinois, Charmer-Sunbelt, Continental Bank, Dean Foods, Exxon-Mobil, First Bank, John Alden Life, Ralph Polo, United Stationers, and University of North Florida.

He has also designed analytics systems for several K-12 public and private school districts across the U.S. to assist them in evaluating the effectiveness of various education programs. His analytic software have been implemented by many leading U.S. school districts.

As a young man, Greg moved to the United States as a political refugee from the former communist empire of the Soviet Union. Since his teenage years in his native Poland, he has always been inspired by the unique American idea of the pursuit of happiness being a foundation of the U.S. Constitution. Greg believes that such a dream can only be achieved via economic and personal freedoms.

Connect with Greg on LinkedIn at
https://www.linkedin.com/in/greggutkowski

Made in the USA
Columbia, SC
28 August 2022

66112689R00183